# BACKSTAIRS LIFE IN A COUNTRY HOUSE

# BACKSTAIRS LIFE IN A COUNTRY HOUSE

**Eileen Balderson**
**with Douglas Goodlad**

DAVID & CHARLES
Newton Abbot London North Pomfret (Vt)

*For Hilda*
*Loved and remembered as a devoted sister and a dedicated cook*

**British Library Cataloguing in Publication Data**

Balderson, Eileen
Backstairs Life In a Country House
1. Servants—Great Britain—history—20th century 2. Country homes—Great Britain—History—20th century
1. Title II. Goodlad, Douglas
640'.46'0924 HD8039.D52.G7

ISBN 0 7153 8021 4

First published 1982
Second impression 1986


Sketches by John Stacey



Photoset by ABM Typographics Limited, Hull
Printed in Great Britain
by A. Wheaton & Co. Ltd, Exeter
for David & Charles Publishers plc
Brunel House Newton Abbot Devon

Published in the United States of America
by David & Charles Inc
North Pomfret Vermont 05053 USA

# Contents

# Conversion Tables

## Oven temperatures

| | | | |
|---|---|---|---|
| Gas Mark | ½ | 250°F | 120°C |
| | 1 | 275°F | 140°C |
| | 2 | 300°F | 150°C |
| | 3 | 325°F | 170°C |
| | 4 | 350°F | 180°C |
| | 5 | 375°F | 190°C |
| | 6 | 400°F | 200°C |
| | 7 | 425°F | 220°C |
| | 8 | 450°F | 230°C |
| | 9 | 475°F | 240°C |

## Liquid measures

(approximate conversions)

| | |
|---|---|
| 1pt (20fl oz) | 570ml |
| ½pt (10fl oz) | 275ml |
| ¼pt (5fl oz) | 150ml |
| 1 mug (8fl oz) | 250ml |
| 1 cup (6fl oz) | 168ml |
| 1 level tablespoon (1fl oz) | 25ml |
| 1 level dessertspoon (½fl oz) | 12ml |
| 1 level teaspoon (1/6fl oz) | 5ml |

## Dry weights

(approximate conversions)

| | |
|---|---|
| 1lb (16oz) | 450g |
| ½lb (8oz) | 225g |
| ¼lb (4oz) | 110g |
| 1oz | 25g |
| | |
| 1 mug (8oz) | 225g |
| 1 cup flour (5oz) | 125g |
| 1 cup rice (6oz) | 175g |
| 1 tablespoon (1oz) | 25g |
| 1 dessertspoon (⅔oz) | 18g |
| 1 teaspoon (⅓oz) | 9g |

# Introduction: Shadow Waltz

It's a plain tale and a true one. The writer claims that this is what being a domestic servant in an English country house in the 1930s was really like. Her account is undramatic and straightforward, but fascinating in its reflection of domestic discipline, customs and attention to detail, and in its insight into high life. It moves from time of depression to wartime, then peace, covering the years from 1931 to the early post-war period.

The story contains no false smile or tear. Not a chair or fork out of place. Not one capless housemaid. Take it, but don't leave it, until you have seen that 'our betters' were not tyrants, fools or gods, but usually worthy providers of good homes for good servants.

Eileen Balderson holds a mirror to life beyond the baize doors, part social calendar and part social history. She is passionately determined to get it right. She says that television series and certain books have got it very wrong. For nearly thirty years she has been an ordinary housewife, now living contentedly in a modest house in the East Midlands. For eleven years before that she lived and worked in country houses of various large sizes.

Meet this practical Yorkshirewoman on a cold evening in her own sitting room where she has made a coal fire, and is allowing the fire, for fancy's sake, to light the room. She has her romantic moments. Firelight can stir her memory into a whirl of colour and sound as shadows dance on the ceiling, on her curtains. An equally effective aide-mémoire is a whiff of hand cream. The dancing light and the fragrance will take her back to the head of the stairs at the hunt ball, with waves of expensive Paris scent drifting towards the roof . . . Somebody else's commodious roof, one of many in her progress from post to post.

These other people's houses were owned by friends of royalty, masters of the hunt, a retired sea captain and a former admiral. Houses big enough to make life seem, at times, one long journey on her knees down stone passages, which she had to scrub. The sandstone she used made that hand cream a necessity, out of a wage of 7s 6d a week.

As the shadows dance, those elegant couples dance again. A red hot coal brings to mind a fuchsia gown or a scarlet one. The men in black and white, mere magpies, but many of the women in brilliant plumage, rare birds of fashion. Eileen has never been made snowblind in a country house, but the colour of the ball gowns is a welcome relief from the predominant white paint. Herself slightly built, she admires the long-stemmed English roses taking the floor, statuesque young ladies who have waltzed out of the pages of Vogue. Each fabulous dress, she imagines, will have cost half the total staff wages for a year.

These are the revellers who will eat the mountain of cocktail sausages prepared by her sister Hilda, the cook. They will be served on sticks. Selling lumber in this much reduced form must be a new way of making money, as novel as the bidets in the front bathrooms.

The band will be served drinks throughout the evening, and she will enjoy weaving among the dancers with her tray. Then she'll get a real whiff of that perfume.

Perfume reminds her of 'the butler who liked to smell nice'. 'He was tall and effeminate, with blond hair he used to smooth with great show, saying "Oh, I do hate these waves. I wish my hair was straight." If he thought no one was looking he pinched and patted the waves into place, to the amusement of us all.'

How did she exchange the simple, scoured doorstep of home for a phalanx of columns and a blaze of windows? How did she make the acquaintance of a creature as rare as a scented butler?

Her first employer was a gentleman, if not gentry, a retired sea captain. He got good value for his five shillings a week. The irony is that it was called a 'morning' job. 'Morning' was 7.30am to 3pm, six days a week, making a forty-five hour week.

She kept 6d pocket money out of her first wage. The other 4s 6d she gave to her sister, who was working minor financial miracles keeping house for her widowed father and the family.

Her mother had died when she was thirteen years old. Her father persuaded her to go into domestic service, urging, 'That way, love, you'll always have a home.' To a sensitive young girl who had lost her mother that made sense. How right he proved to be, for the Depression was glowering round the corner, and living with the gentry was an enviable form of security.

The Drewerys of St George's Road, Hull, if a little less elevated, were a pleasant family who supplemented that first wage with breakfast and dinner. She felt, in her small way, that she was helping her own family.

About a year later, after considering work in a department store or in an hotel, she began her country house career, her progress from one stately home of England to another.

'The only thing we lacked was freedom,' says Eileen Balderson, as if 'imprisonment' in a big house was of small consequence.

'We were disciplined, regimented, labelled, restricted, but we also had a lot of fun, good food and lodging, and even some perks and privileges.

'Those in charge were stern, even frightening. We were even in awe of the unknown, since the master was a remote figure rarely seen by some of us. But among servants at my level I made many good friends, and at one of my "places" I had a "secret romance" with the (odourless) butler!'

What follows is her accurate image of country house life in

the thirties produced from a photographic memory. The book also allows readers literally to recapture the flavour of the thirties in a big country house by trying some of the recipes (the less expensive ones, perhaps) quoted from the handwritten cookery book of the writer's sister. Recipes as varied as those for aspic jelly, lobster cream and sloe gin are included in the final chapters. They are taken from the cookery book now in the possession of the writer's brother-in-law, who was the butler at a house where her sister was cook.

# 1
# Sisters in Service

I was born in Hull, the youngest of a family of nine. I left school at fourteen. I was lucky at my first country house to be with my sister Hilda, who was experienced, with an exemplary domestic career, and was also loving and caring towards the family, a rock to us all. She left home when mother died to return to Rise Park, near Hornsea, where she had been kitchenmaid. My other sister Edith, a few years older than I was, took over our housekeeping.

Hilda was a marvellous comfort to me in my first job away from Hull and home. She had packed her trunk for a second time because she did not wish to strain our family resources, and she knew that Edith was very capable of taking charge. Hilda was now cook-housekeeper at Rise, playing a double role. Saki's famous line, 'The cook was a good cook, as good cooks go; and as cooks go she went', has often been echoed in country households. The cook at Rise Park went because of a reduction in the number of staff.

The year was 1931. Depression had thrown 2½ million out of work, and even the gentry were having to cut expenses. The owner of Rise Park house and estate cut his staff from sixteen to eleven indoors and closed part of the house.

The nursery staff of three was reduced to one. There had

been a governess nanny, an under-nurse and a nursery-maid. Only the under-nurse was kept on. The butler was dispensed with, so the footman took over his duties and the hall boy became footman. The housemaid and kitchen staffs were reduced to two and a between-maid was employed. Hilda took over from the old cook. The mistress's personal maid and the chauffeur remained. The 'quality' were well looked after even when staff numbers had been cut. How many butlers do you know today?

I was offered the post of between-maid. I had on several occasions visited Hilda at this house when she herself was the kitchen maid, and I liked the look of it. Rise was a house in the Adam style. The owner was Captain Adrian Bethell. I have many delightful recollections of the flowers on the estates where I worked and I remember Captain Bethell for his white carnation. He always wore one as a buttonhole. I don't remember much more about him. The master of a country house was usually only a shadowy figure to most servants.

I thought, rightly, that it would be splendid to work at Rise because my duties as tweeny would be divided between work with the housemaids and with my sister in the kitchen. I was fifteen and a half and my weekly wage was 7s 6d.

Distraction from the Depression in 1931 included the exploits of a typist from a solicitor's office who flew solo towards Pekin at the beginning of the year. She got as far as Berlin. Her name was Amy Johnson, and she was a Hull girl, like me. In 1930, at the age of twenty-six, 'wonderful Amy' had made her nineteen-day solo flight to Australia.

Charlie Chaplin came to London for the première of his picture *City Lights,* which glorified the tramp-like character he played, and gave him the common touch in days of Depression. There were plenty of unemployed around less well dressed than his tramp!

Mrs Ernest Simpson, who was presented at Court, did not match the mood of the times quite so well. Nor did Lord Fitzwilliam's big St Leger party at Wentworth Woodhouse, where the guests included one who used luminous paint for her finger nails. What my capable sister had at her finger-tips was far more admirable, thought this particular tweeny.

My sister died in 1979 while this book was being written. I know she would have endorsed what I have to say about service in a country house. I hope she would have been proud of the final result.

* * * *

Books about domestic service mostly concern London houses and upper middle class families. The television series, *Upstairs Downstairs* and *The Duchess of Duke Street* dealt with that type of household.

Life in a large country house was vastly different, both for the gentry and the staff. My eleven years in this setting were, in the main, very happy.

Domestic servants are said to have been exploited. I do not agree. Exploitation applied much more to other workers. Wages were poor whatever the form of employment. At the same time prices were low and quality of goods high.

Girls had to move from house to house to progress. Head servants in good houses never left, the conditions were so satisfactory. Girls sought advancement through domestic agencies, always asking for a bigger wage than they expected to get.

There was no need for a girl to stay where conditions were poor. Good domestic agencies (there were many in London and most large towns) had a black list of employers who could not keep staff, and also of unreliable workers. I was told not to apply for any job advertised in a newspaper, since resorting to newspaper advertising showed the mistress was not very good to work for! At one time I had the idea that I would like to work as a chambermaid in an hotel, but I was told that there would be difficulty in obtaining a post in good service afterwards.

A girl in good service usually had a comfortable bedroom, even if it was shared with another girl. This was often the case with under-maids. When girls were together in a room, they were not cramped for space and each girl had her own dressing table, set of drawers, wardrobe, wash-stand, chair and bed.

Bedrooms were mostly carpeted. According to the size of the household there would be a servants' hall, housekeeper's room, housemaids' sitting room; but always a servants' hall, if not the other two sitting rooms. These were sometimes carpeted, and they had armchairs, a sofa and a good fire, with unlimited fuel in the winter.

In the early 1930s, before the tranny and hi-fi, not many radios were provided. In one audio-conscious house where I worked, there was a gramophone and records and later a radio.

One daily and one Sunday newspaper were delivered for the servants' hall. All periodicals such as *Punch*, *Tatler*, *Illustrated London News* were passed on from the front of the house. The two regions of a country house were always known as 'the front' and 'the back', as opposed to the 'upstairs' and 'downstairs' of London houses.

Food on the whole was good and plentiful, depending, in some cases, on the cook. As most estates had a home farm, all dairy produce was in ample supply. Often they killed their own beef, lamb and pork. There was also game in the shooting season. What game the servants' hall got varied from house to house.

No girl had her own washing or ironing to do, since clothes were either sent to a local laundry, or laundry-maids were employed.

In some houses bicycles were provided for staff use. When 'everything found' was taken into consideration, domestic work compared favourably with other employment. Head servants had a fire in their bedrooms in the winter, those of lesser degree were expected to be hardier!

To my mind the only thing we lacked was freedom, and even that wasn't so terrible. Some shop and factory girls worked long hours, and shop girls for very low wages. What use was a lot of free time if one could not afford outings or entertainment?

An estate worker, a gardener, groom or woodman, for instance, was better off than some of the staff. He usually had a cottage, with very often a good garden where he could grow fruit and vegetables. In many cases he kept a few chickens and a pig. Milk was often provided daily, and such workers could expect the odd rabbit or hare during the shooting season. So again, compared with a town worker who had everything to buy out of a low wage, the domestic was fortunate.

The gentry mostly had the welfare of their workers in mind. In the case of one house in which I worked, the lady used to visit the wives in their cottages. Certainly in times of trouble most were anxious to give practical help.

When an old employee retired, he and his wife were often allowed to remain in their cottage and in some cases a small pension was provided.

* * * *

A Yorkshire servant, trying a country house for size, might measure it against Wentworth Woodhouse, the residence of Earl Fitzwilliam, and the largest private house in England. It is now the 'seat' of teacher training.

The house, near Rotherham, has 365 windows on its frontage, and guests used to be given packets of wafers or some such means of leaving a trail if they wandered about the premises. The grounds were big enough to accommodate open-cast coal-mining, which was carried out there for some years. In the days when the Rockingham pottery flourished near by, vases and jugs bigger than a man were commissioned as space fillers. When one of the jugs was filled with punch, lifting for pouring was the work of at least a couple of servants.

I was overwhelmed by such size. The biggest establishment I was to serve in was Lord Boyne's Burwarton House. It was vast, terribly isolated, and we were much more regimented than elsewhere. I preferred smaller houses where we were more like a family. I stayed six months!

Rise Park was big enough in all conscience. I got lost on my first week there. I would have felt stupid if I'd asked my way!

May I show you round? I remember the large front hall, marvellous for making an entrance. Although for economy reasons many of the rooms were closed, the rooms in use were so numerous and so varied in their purpose that there is small wonder I was bewildered to begin with, and that I had only 'passing acquaintance' with some rooms. The house was big enough for accommodation to be offered for Women's Institute and Mothers' Union meetings in the 'guild room' before the village hall was built.

Rooms, rooms, rooms! Flowers had a room of their own, the flower hall with glass doors leading to one of the many lawns. I recall chrysanthemums taller than me. Flower arranging was a male responsibility. Mr Alderman, the head gardener, used to attend to the flowers.

Servants had their meals together in the housekeeper's room. The boot hall where shoes and riding boots were cleaned was huge and paved with stone. The knife-cleaning machines were located there. Leading off the boot hall was a room where men's suits and hunting clothes were cleaned, and the gun room was in this area.

I do not wish the reader to get lost as I was with too detailed a geography of the house, but I should mention the four larders, the first with prepared food and ice boxes (more to come about those), and the next where carcases of lamb and sides of beef were cut up. The third seemed to be a general dump and this was where Peggy the kitchen-maid and myself collected my bath—yes, bath!—of potatoes every evening. We took a handle each in carrying it away. Fourth was the game larder.

There were baths for people as well as for potatoes. The furnace room supplied the water. There were two big furnaces, one for domestic hot water, the other for central heating. Each furnace was large enough for me to lie down in and high enough to kneel in—though I never tried either!

The room of most personal significance was the large bedroom which Emma, the second housemaid, and I shared with Peggy. End of the climb to Bedfordshire was just six wooden stairs from the landing, but sometimes counted wearily.

Heart or hub of the house was the main staircase of stone. Opposite the stairs was the serving hall, the still room (where liquors and preserves were kept and tea prepared), the butler's pantry and the dining room, which had one door for the food and another for the family! Leading off the serving hall was Mrs Bethell's sitting room, but this did not mean constant interference from the mistress. Indeed, for most of the day she kept out of the way of the cook. I am sure that Hilda had no love of power, but as cook was expected to wield it.

In most houses the mistress went to the kitchen at 10am to pass the menu. The menu slate and pencil were put ready on a small table with a white cloth, and a chair by the table. She approved or altered the menu as she wished, and discussed any other items with the cook. Once she had left the kitchen, she would not return that day. Any communication would be sent by the footman. If she did go to the kitchen later, which was rarely, she knocked on the door and waited for cook to say 'Come in'.

Finding my way about the house in those first weeks was like playing a Victorian board game. Imagine the colourful board with its picture of the park and deer, lake and ducks, and the house drawn roofless to display the interior and the disposition of the rooms.

Throw a six and advance to the housekeeper's room for staff dinner (this would no doubt be represented on the appropriate square by a large tureen emitting cumulus clouds of steam). Can you imagine the various obstacles? Go back to menservants' sitting room, miss three throws for a sit down. Go to men's wooden stairs. Miss several throws through having to scrub them to a shining whiteness.

To the 'slide' (a very large hatch) to help the footman with the meal, bonus of ten squares. Or for a penalty you might have to make a detour via the kitchen-maid's white-scrubbed stairs. Other throws could have you penalised by scrubbing in the housemaids' pantry or the maids' bathroom, or there might be hazards in the nursery wing. 'Go back to Master Tony's room.' (He has been sick on the carpet.)

I have left out of the game the smallest 'staff room' in this area. It had a scrubbed white contemplative seat and a handle pulled upwards to flush. That room could have made one of the 'stop' squares in the game, a pause to reflect on the benefits and an opportunity to flush away problems of country house life.

And what about that huge room where you had lots of space to dance and see yourself reflected over and over? It had many big windows and between them were tall mirrors. These were along two sides of the room, the ballroom. How many affairs and romances began there, I wonder.

* * * *

What dress for the job? A housemaid's uniform consisted of a striped print dress, usually blue and white, but pink or mauve and white were sometimes worn. She wore a large white apron and a cap. For afternoons in the larger households a black dress with the same apron and cap as in the morning. In some smaller households the housemaids wore a small fancy apron and cap with the black dress.

Some mistresses preferred a brown dress and ecru apron and cap. In this case it was usually provided. A blue drill apron was often worn over the white morning one for 'rough work' such as cleaning grates and scrubbing floors. Black shoes and stockings were always worn.

A cook usually dressed completely in white. Either a white dress and apron or white skirt and blouse with white apron. A cap was not compulsory, neither was it for a head housemaid.

A butler's morning wear was usually a soft white shirt, black tie, black waistcoat and jacket with pin-striped trousers and black laced shoes and socks. He changed at lunchtime into a morning coat. In the evenings he wore full evening dress—black trousers braided down the outside seams, tail coat, patent leather shoes or pumps, a black dress waistcoat, a stiff white shirt and white bow tie, except if there were guests so attired. Then to distinguish him from them he would wear a white dress waistcoat and black bow tie.

Where a large staff was kept, the footman wore in the morning a single breasted lounge suit in either charcoal grey or the family livery colour. The bright buttons bore the family crest. During the afternoon and evening livery was worn. This was similar to an evening dress suit except that it fastened with link buttons, crested. The colour was blue, bottle green or maroon. The waistcoat, cut evening style, was of livery cloth or linen, vertically or horizontally striped in black and yellow, bottle green and yellow or blue and white. When in livery the footman wore a stiff dress shirt with wing collar and white dress tie.

Livery for the house itself was white. I must have seen many acres of white paint indoors during my service.

In most houses the first footman slept in a room off the butler's pantry where the silver safe was kept. In one house where I worked the footman had a truncheon hanging on the head of his bed, for possible use on intruders. In a London house the menservants slept in the basement and the maids in the attics. In a large country house they were in separate wings.

In some large houses morning prayers were held in the dining room, led by the master and mistress. Any guests who remembered and came down to breakfast in time, and any servants who could be spared from work also attended usually housemaids and pantry staff.

There was a certain amount of protocol, mostly, I think of the head servants' making. A cook was always given the title of 'Mrs', even if, as in most cases, she was a single person. Personal maids, butlers, chauffeurs, heads of outside staff were known by surname only. All under staff were addressed by their Christian names.

Newspapers sometimes came by post, especially *The Times* and *The Morning Post*. They were taken out of their wrappers and carefully pressed with an iron to remove all the creases before being taken to the front of the house.

This was the land of green baize, which even invaded the safe where the silver was kept. The safe's shelves were baize-covered.

The safe, about 6ft square, was in the butler's pantry. It was, in effect, a small strong room with shelves on three sides. Entrée dishes, silver sauce boats, salvers and candlesticks were kept in green baize bags. The butler and footman wore baize aprons when cleaning silver, but a white linen one for washing the glass.

Often, where there was a door leading from the back quarters to the front, it would be covered both sides with baize. At Rise Park the night nurseries had double doors. The intention was to keep out noise when the children were sleeping.

# 2
# Now, Madam!

The cook was a law unto herself and no mistake. A family was expected to abide by certain unwritten rules, particularly rules of punctuality. If they were just occasionally a little late for a meal, and it had to be held up a few minutes, nothing would be said. If, however, this happened too frequently, the mistress was told about it.

Cook said firmly, 'Now madam, will you try to be more punctual for your meals? I can't produce a good meal if it's to be kept waiting . . .'

A mistress respected her cook, and was at pains not to offend, since she put her status where her own mouth and those of her guests were. An excellent cook gave much-valued superiority.

Likewise, if she wanted to take the children out, she always asked Nanny if it would be convenient, and Nanny usually went with them, so the children were still in her charge, and the mother would not think of going against her word. Where there was a schoolroom and lessons to be done, the word of the governess was just as strictly followed.

Wherever we went about the house together, such as to meals or to do the lunch and dinnertime tidying, the housemaids—Alice, Emma and myself—walked in single file; as we approached a door, I had to walk forward, open it, and stand aside while they passed through.

The same applied to seating at the servants' hall table; butler at the head of the table, my sister, cook-housekeeper at the foot. On her left, lady's maid, kitchen-maid and myself; on the butler's left, footman, chauffeur, Emma, Alice, the old head housemaid, and so back to my sister, Hilda. The meal was also served in the order of one's position in the household. There was a lot of protocol and a strict code of behaviour was observed. This also applied to the family.

My duties as a tweeny were to work with the housemaids until 12 noon, then go the kitchen for the rest of the day. My escape to the kitchen and my sister, whom I loved very much, never came quickly enough. Alice was very strict and I was more than a little afraid of her.

Alice was about fifty, and she seemed very old and fierce to a young girl. She had been with the family for years and she did not count a day complete unless she had found a complaint, something not cleaned properly or some other minor fault.

She was very fat and sat queen-like in a Windsor chair with a footstool, waiting for the next thing to criticise. With my fellow housemaid Emma I used to sit on the steps near the housemaids' pantry—and whisper. Alice told us off loudly and her humiliating tongue made us feel inadequate and ignorant.

Looking back, I realise she needed to be strict, to train a young girl to do her work properly. She was probably quite a nice person, and had I worked with her a few years later after a little training, she would not have seemed so fierce. Certainly, the second housemaid, who was several years older than me, got on very well with her. I was very shy and timid in those days and no doubt like all youngsters didn't always do my work quite up to standard.

We rose at 6am every morning, even on Sundays. We had one half day off duty per week, and a half day alternate Sundays. Our half day started when we had finished our morning duties. The time we went off duty varied according to whether there were guests in the house, and how much work they involved. If we wanted to go into Hull or Hornsea and hurried with our work, we could be 'off' by 2.30pm. On the other hand it could be 3pm and we had to be back in at 10pm. We were in dire trouble if we returned late.

If Mrs Bethell happened to be going into Hull, she would send a message round the staff that there would be a lift for anyone who wished to go.

My first job in the winter was to clean the grates and lay the fires in Mrs Bethell's private sitting room, the estate office and day nursery. All were black-leaded, with fenders and fire irons of brass or steel. The steel was polished with emery paper and a burnisher (a piece of leather about 4in square covered with steel mesh). Brass polish was made by the head housemaid. I think it was a mixture of bath brick and turpentine. She also made the floor and furniture polish from beeswax and turpentine.

The hearths in the day nursery and estate office were of stone, kept bright with a whitener. When cleaned with the hearth stone, they had the appearance of having been whitewashed. All other fireplaces in the downstairs rooms and many 'front' bathrooms were of white marble, most of which were beautifully carved.

Floors were polished with a tool called a jumbo. As the name implies, this was very heavy, its weight imparting the polish. It consisted of a wedge-shaped piece of wood on a long handle. This was the only house in which I ever came across such a contrivance. The wood was weighted with lead, with a felt pad on one side and bristles on the other. It was as much as I could lift, and when pushing it backwards and forwards over the floor, I nearly went with it, flat on my back. I was a small featherweight in those days.

Brushing carpets by hand made clouds of dust all round. We waved dusters out of windows to produce more pother.

For cleaning fireplaces we had a square box full of tools. It was made of wood or tin. A sectional tray fitted on the top containing the black-lead brushes, small sweeping brush, shovel and all our polishes. We also had a large hessian sheet about 2yd by 1yd which we spread over the carpet in front of the fireplace to keep it clean while the grate was receiving attention. The box beneath the tray contained sticks for laying fires, and when the sticks were removed the ashes from the grates were substituted, to be emptied later into the ash pit in the scullery yard. The hessian sheet went to the laundry each week so that it was always clean and in good condition.

After the grates, I had to sweep and dust the estate office. There were no vacuum cleaners. All carpets were either brushed with a long-handled, stiff carpet broom or a small stiff brush and dustpan. The whalebone bristles created a lot of dust, so dusting was a big job.

A long stone paved passage led from the estate office to the serving hall. This I also had to sweep and dust. Once a week I had to scrub this floor with scouring stone and a scrubbing brush. The stone used was a rough piece of sandstone. After cleaning the passage, I had to sweep and dust the nursery stairs and hall, from which a door led out to a side drive used by the nanny and the children, Christopher and Hugh. We always referred to Nanny as Nursery Alice, since the head housemaid was also called Alice.

All the downstairs rooms had to be cleaned before the dining room breakfast, which was at 9am. The staff breakfast was at 8am. A bell was rung for all staff meals. It was quite a size, hanging in its tower above the still room windows. We used to open one of the windows to pull the rope. As it was my job to serve staff tea every day and supper on the footman's half day off I had to ring the bell and it was very heavy. I was less than 5ft tall, so reaching the rope through the window was precarious, and I must have produced a very queer ring! The bell could be heard at Skirlaugh, about a mile away, and I wondered what the villagers thought of my efforts. I expect some of them told the time by the chimes of the stable clock in its tower over the stable archway.

At other times when the second housemaid and I heard the bell we went to the housemaids' pantry, where we were joined by Alice. We dared not go to a meal without her. Neither dared we leave the table without her permission. When she put down her knife and fork, we had to do the same, whether we had finished our meal or not! A legacy of those days is that I still eat quickly, even though no one is waiting to whisk my plate away.

After breakfast, Emma and I made all the staff beds, and I had all staff bedrooms and maids' bathroom to clean, as well as the male servants' wing, consisting of butler's, footman's and chauffeur's rooms, spare rooms for when there were visiting male servants, together with their bathroom, quite a cleaning marathon.

Water, water, everywhere! There were no wash basins in bedrooms but wash stands, with a wash bowl and a large jug always kept full of clean cold water, soap dish, toothbrush holder, glass tumbler and carafe filled with fresh clean drinking water every day. These were in every bedroom in the house, both in the back-quarters and the front.

Captain Bethell's ablutions were special. In the housemaids' pantry was a fireplace with a small hob at one side and a boiler on the other, which was filled every day with rainwater from a rain barrel by the scullery door. This soft water was for the captain's shaving, and the butler took a brass can full to his dressing room every morning when he was called, and in the evening when laying out the captain's evening clothes. Adult members of the family and visitors were always called with a can of hot water to wash with and a tray of tea, usually with petit beurre biscuits, though in a case of a visitor, wafer-thin bread and butter, a speciality of Rise, might be preferred.

There was always a tin of biscuits in every bedroom. Each guest room had a writing desk with blotter, headed notepaper, pen and ink and a selection of books to read.

Headservants were always called with a cup of tea and can of hot washing water. If they wished, they had a bedroom fire in the winter—more cleaning, and the fire to lay ready for lighting.

We had a kettle in the housemaids' pantry for filling hot water bottles in the winter, both for the family and for head servants. This was always our last duty at night. Housemaids also made their own tea for mid-morning break in their own pantry. I had to keep the cake tin, sugar and tea replenished from the kitchen.

At one end of the housemaids' pantry was a small coal house where coal and firewood for all bedroom fires were kept. Coal used to be hauled up on a pulley through a door high up on the wall of the 'men's yard' by the lorryman, Jeffries. Two steps led down to the coal house from the housemaids' pantry, with a low wall across it to keep the coal in a tidy heap. The steps were kept whitened!

Once a week I had the linen room to scrub out. This was a moderately sized room with heated cupboards from floor to ceiling on two sides, where all the household linen was kept. The huge hampers in which the linen was sent to the laundry were kept there. Some of the linen was very old, beautifully fine and the 'turn down' of the top sheets and pillow cases delicately embroidered, or edged with fine handmade lace. Hand towels were either huckaback linen or very fine linen, also embroidered or lace edged. Staff always had two huckaback hand towels and a huge bath towel each.

All staff clothes went to the laundry, both uniform and personal clothes such as my dresses. The only things we washed ourselves were stockings. We had a laundry book each, to enter all articles in. This, with our washing made into a bundle, had to be on the linen room table by 10am every Friday and the clean washing collected from there on the same afternoon. It was all paid for by our employers.

I was paid 7s 6d a week at Rise Park, but I had no expenses. Everything I needed apart from clothes was provided.

# 3
# From Shutters to Scullery

Remember Mrs Gamp on shutters? 'We never know wot's hidden in each other's hearts; and if we had glass winders there, we'd need to keep the shutters up, some on us, I do assure you!'

Mrs Gamp has it quite correctly, I am sure. I wonder what she would have thought of the actual shutters at Rise. I can see her brandishing her famous umbrella at them, indeed, pouring her heart out about them, which is how I felt frequently.

Every room and most passages and halls throughout the house were fitted with shutters to the windows. Some folded back into a recess at the sides of the windows, others pulled upwards from a cavity beneath the windowsill and were secured with a bolt through two holes in the centre of both shutters. The side folding ones were fastened with an iron bar. Most rooms also had curtains and some had blinds as well, so shutting up and opening out in the morning was quite a job. A few of the outer doors of the house had iron bars across them in addition to huge bolts at the top and bottom, also a key often about 6in long—not one to carry in one's pocket!

The windows at the front of the house, both upstairs and down, were fitted with sunblinds outside. They were similar to a venetian blind, with slats made of canvas. It was the housemaid's job to see that all sunblinds were down in sunny weather on all upstairs windows.

I had all the servants' rooms to sweep and dust with the exception of my sister's. It was the practice in most houses for the kitchen-maid to do the cook's room. A pity, since I would have loved to have been responsible for Hilda's room.

What joy to get to my adored sister and away from Alice. I remember her once asking me to do something and I didn't hear and said 'What?' If I had sworn at her she couldn't have been more affronted. 'Don't you "what" me.' 'Beg your pardon, Alice.' It had to be 'Alice' after everything I said to her. 'Yes, Alice.' 'No Alice.' 'Three bags full, Alice.'

The scullery where I did most of my afternoon and evening work was a very large room leading from an enormous kitchen. Both were stone-paved, the same as the larders and a long passage leading to them. A stone staircase led to the game larder where, in the shooting season, was all the game—pheasants, partridge, woodcock, snipe, rabbits, hares. There were three big windows along one side, unglazed but covered on the inside with fine galvanized mesh and on the outer frame with wooden louvres, leaving a space of several inches between the two. In the Spring, wood pigeons used to nest on the windowsill in this space.

In the middle of the larder was a wooden chest into which the kitchen-maid plucked the birds. At the end of the shooting season, the feathers were sold and each week throughout the season a man called for the rabbit and hare skins. The money from these sales was always regarded as the kitchen-maid's perks.

I am glad I never was kitchen-maid because I was petrified at the thought of skinning animals or plucking hens. Yes, I was glad to be a tweeny, especially as any tear in a rabbit skin meant trouble.

Washing up was daunting. Under the scullery window was a large sandstone sink. To the right of this fixed to the wall, was a long plate rack, 6ft by 4ft, with a draining board underneath. For washing up I used two zinc baths about the size of a clothes basket, one with hot soapy water and the other with clear water for rinsing, then all plates and dishes were put into the rack to drain. There were no washing up liquids in those days. Soft soap was used for everything except pans, and soda was used for them.

It was the footman's job to put plates and dishes to warm, for the dining room, nursery and servants' hall. As he took each plate from the rack, he polished it with a clean glass cloth. Menus for the three sections of the house were written on a slate. The footman had to look at it to know what plates to put up to warm and what to lay the tables for. At 7pm each evening, he brought the menu slates to the kitchen for my sister to write. They were white porcelain with the front roughened for writing on. All dinner menus (not lunch) were written in French.

The plates and dishes were warmed in a rack over the kitchen range. A sliding shutter covered the warming compartment to prevent them getting dusty. The kitchen range was a huge black-leaded and steel one, polished every morning. It would be about 4ft long with a central fire box and an oven at each side. When the kitchen-maid made up the fire, any pans on the top of the stove were lifted off, unless they had lids on.

One evening my sister let me wash a few cooking utensils at the kitchen sink as it was winter time and cold in the scullery. A pan that had got burnt had been put at the side of the stove to soak, and the water had turned brown. The kitchen-maid took two pans off and put them on the draining board to make up the fire. Thinking I would have a go at the burnt pan, I threw the water down the sink and was busy scratching away. The footman, Ronald, was waiting to take in the soup when Hilda started shouting, 'Where's my soup. Where's my soup?' I knew instantly what I had done. I had thrown the Consommé Julienne down the sink! I fled from the kitchen up to her bedroom and when the panic was over, she found me sitting on the rug in front of her fire weeping. As always she was very sweet and told me everything was all right and to go back downstairs. It was apparently her last drop of Consommé Julienne, so she had to heat some other kind. There were usually several kinds on the go at one time. Ronald brought back the menu slates to alter the name of the soup. What she told Mrs Bethell the following morning, I don't know.

The kitchen range was an 'Eagle', a very well-known make at that time. Each time it was made up, it took a full scuttle of coal. There was at the side of this another very old range, not used in my time, with a spit hanging from a huge iron bracket fixed in the wall above. Later this was bricked up and one of the first Agas ever on the market was installed. It looked impossibly small after the 'Eagle'.

My first job on reaching the scullery was to wash all cooking utensils used during the morning. Nursery and servants' hall dinner was at 12.30pm, dining room lunch at 1.30pm. I had all the plates and dishes to wash from the three meals. Glasses and silver were washed in the butler's pantry. Emma washed the nursery dishes in the nursery pantry.

The pans were either of copper or of cast iron. The iron ones were very heavy and some of the big ones as much as I could lift empty. The copper pans and jelly moulds, flan rings and the rest were polished by a woman who came in from the village once a week. Silver sand and vinegar rubbed on with the hands, then washed off and polished with a cloth was the usual method.

The copper pans and moulds were on long shelves, the pans one side and the moulds on the other side of the kitchen door, where they gleamed in soldierly array.

Scrubbing was a way of life. After washing up, I scrubbed the scullery tables and tidied the room. The kitchen-maid gave the kitchen tables the same attention, as well as scrubbing a strip of the kitchen floor in front of the range, after doing the flues, black-leading and lighting the range! The sinks in the kitchen and butler's pantry were wooden ones, lead-lined. This was usual in most big houses.

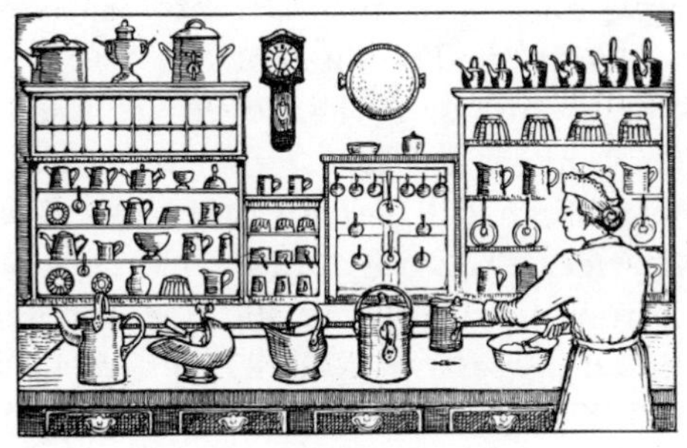

# 4
# Work with a Song

My 'morning' duties were finished by 2.30pm or 3pm, depending on how many people were in the dining room and how many courses they had. Staff and nursery lunch usually consisted of two courses. There were three courses for dining room lunch, and for dinner there were four or five courses and dessert, unless guests were being entertained, when there could be as many as eight courses. Whatever the dining room had for lunch, there was always a cold ham and tongue on the sideboard.

There was the servants' hall tea to serve and the dishes to wash. The drawing room tea dishes were washed in the butler's pantry. I had about ¾cwt potatoes to peel for the next day.

I used to sing while peeling. One of my favourites was 'Little Grey Home in the West'. I knew how many potatoes I could peel per verse and chorus! But I had many other 'spud peelers', learned from Hilda. They included 'I Dreamt that I Dwelt in Marble Halls', 'The Rose of Tralee', 'Songs of Araby', 'Indian Love Lyrics', 'I Passed by Your Window', 'Absent' and 'A Brown Bird Singing'.

If cooking salt was needed in the kitchen, I had a 7lb block to rub through a sieve, which was a painful job if my hands were chapped, as they often were in the winter. After these jobs came all the washing up again. Servants' hall supper was at 9pm, so I usually finished about 10pm.

I was very happy at Rise Park. I loved the house and its surroundings, and being with my sister made all the difference.

It is sad, but true, that all was not always sweet for the young in domestic service. It was not unknown for a girl occasionally to run away from a place where she was unhappy or under pressure from an aggressive head servant, especially a cook. Rather than suffer further aggression by serving a month's notice she would hop it.

The young girl who was scullery maid at Rise when Hilda was kitchen-maid ran away. Hilda shared a room with her and awoke one morning to find she had left a note beside Hilda's bed, and gone. She left her luggage behind, but took her rabbit skins. She knew her luggage would be sent on, but not the rabbit skins and these represented money to her. Why she ran away no one was sure but one incident occurred which may have been the last straw.

She was asked to dress some snipe and had been shown how, but must have forgotten. She treated the snipe like most other birds by plucking and cutting off legs and head, and drawing it. When the Irish cook saw it she went beserk and made her put back the innards and sew the legs and head back on, saying that would teach her to remember in future!

A snipe should be plucked, and only the gizzard removed. It has to be skinned and the eyes removed, the head brought round and the long beak put through where wings and legs cross. When cooked it is served on a piece of toast, one bird per person, usually as a savoury.

When I was later working for the Hellyers at Middleton Hall the kitchen-maid ran away one dark night. She was sent out to the dairy for some cream, but never returned. It was assumed that she must have hidden her coat and case there waiting for the right moment. It was all hushed up and I never heard why she did it.

One can understand a young girl, fourteen or fifteen years old, miles away from home in some cases for the first time finding the pressures of work and headservants intolerable.

Such were the rigours of domestic service training and discipline, particularly in the kitchen. I was indeed fortunate to be working with my sister in my early days in service.

On the kitchen-maid's half day, I had minor jobs to do like making toast. No electric toaster—it was made in front of the kitchen range on a long toasting fork. Butter was never served in the dining room at lunch and dinner in a 'piece'. It was made into small marble-sized balls. About three were put on a small, crystal dish topped with a sprig of parsley, one dish for each person. I had these butter balls to make with a pair of 'scotch hands', which is more difficult than it sounds. I sometimes managed points on the top!

Parsley was used a lot, in the garnishing of cold meats especially. The kitchen table had to be 'laid up' in readiness for the cooking of the dinner, which was usually served at 8pm. There had to be a pile of enamel plates, basins, mixing bowls, two or three chopping boards, metal and wooden spoons of varying sizes, knives and cooking forks, seasoning, and anything else I thought Hilda might require. She was a most efficient cook, and I found some of her dishes most fascinating to watch in the making. Many, such as cream of chicken or salmon moulds were most beautifully garnished, and required much skill, time and patience.

Hilda's presentation of salmon was a true work of art. She garnished a whole salmon with aspic, truffles and flowers made out of vegetables. I declare a salmon would leap for joy at the prospect of appearing in the party dress Hilda would provide for him!

In those days there were no tinned soups and none of the present-day packeted foods. Everything was home-made, including aspic jelly and brown glaze to garnish ham and tongue.

Everything in the grocery and cleaning line was bought in bulk; soft soap in hundredweight barrels; soda, flour, sugar in hundredweight sacks. Scrubbing soap was White Primrose in 2ft bars and, cut after being in store a while, became rock hard. A traveller used to come out from Field's grocery store in Hull once a week to take the order and it was delivered later in the week.

All fruit and vegetables were supplied from the extensive kitchen gardens. The head gardener came each morning to see what was required for the day.

Jenkins, the cowman, brought milk and cream every morning and late afternoon. Eggs, butter made at the home farm and poultry were ordered as required. The Bethells killed their own beef, mutton, venison and pork and all bacon and ham was home-cured.

Monday was store day. The under-servant from each department wrote a list of what was needed and found receptacles. Housemaids required dusters, toilet and hard soap, a jar of soft soap, a tin of soda, black-lead and all cleaning materials. The lists and jars were put on a table outside the store room next door to Hilda's room by 10am and collected from there later in the day. If we forgot an item we needed, we had to wait until the next week. The store room was unlocked for dispensing stores only once a week.

Coal for the house came direct from the mine to Skirlaugh station. When the estate office was informed of its arrival, Jeffries, the lorryman, had to cart and unload it into the coal house in the scullery yard. He also had coke to cart from Hull gas works for the furnaces. Even in those days a large part of the house was centrally heated. It was part of Ronald's duties to keep the furnaces stoked. He had done this when he was hall boy and continued when he became footman. Another of Jeffries' duties was to cart any luggage to or from the station for maids as required, and fruit, vegetables and game for sale to Plummers, who were poulterers, game dealers and greengrocers. He also brought the hundredweight blocks of ice for the ice boxes.

An extensive kitchen garden produced all fruit and vegetables for the house and exquisite plants and flowers, which Alderman (the head gardener) attended to every morning. It was the practice in all big houses for two gardeners to go into the house every morning before dining-room breakfast to replace dead flowers and plants with fresh ones and do the watering. The gardeners arranged the flowers better than most women so-called experts. There were enormous greenhouse flowers all the year round. Handsome laburnums and lilacs were in tubs in the rooms.

The estate was beautifully maintained, as were all big estates in East Yorkshire. Fields were either fenced or hedged, never this awful ranching which is now spoiling lovely countryside. All field gates were painted white, with the gentleman's initials in black in the middle of the top rail. Once a year the tenant farmer paid their rent at the estate office and a meal was always provided for them in the men's hall. Links we had with the village of Skirlaugh included the stable clock—the chimes could be heard across the park and woods—and Rise Church, small and pretty, standing within the grounds, and reached via the laurel walk.

The stables had a special attraction for me. The loose boxes were built around the stable yard, and what a pride the grooms took in them. The lower half of each was varnished, tongued and grooved boards. Black enamelled, vertical rails formed the upper half and door. All hasps and door fastenings were of brass and always beautifully polished. The doorsteps into the loose boxes and the saddle room were scrubbed and whitened with a hearth stone. All the riding tack, bridles, reins and saddles were kept there.

There used to be a regular joke played on any new stable lad who arrived. It was a favourite jest of the footman, who said to him, 'Captain Bethell would like the saddle horse taking round to the front door.' The saddle horse was a wooden structure on which the saddles were cleaned and polished!

In comparison with life in the hall with its large staff and innumerable rooms, the estate workers appeared to be only playing house in their cottages, attractively situated in parkland, but doll's houses against Rise itself.

The scullery yard was cobbled with round stones, as all the yards were. There was an open shed in the yard in which a few bantam hens were kept as pets, and two peahens and a peacock.

If the peafowl wandered down to the village, they were quickly driven back as the village people said they were unlucky. They could certainly be destructive. I kept out of their way. They were too noisy and aggressive for me.

One morning, Lily, Mrs Bethell's personal maid, told us at breakfast that she was awakened in the night by the sound of breaking glass as the stable clock struck 2am. All very dramatic—and suggesting a visit by burglars. She was much teased by the male servants about this, who thought it might be wishful thinking!

However, one afternoon I was emptying the ashes from my hearth box when I heard a crash of breaking glass. One of the peahens was standing on the windowsill of a spare staff bedroom pecking at the window panes and breaking them!

Two lodges which held great appeal for me were the gamekeeper's cottage set in a clearing on the edge of the wood along the Skirlaugh road. Further along was the woodman's cottage. From here was a 'ride' through the wood to the park and lake. In the opposite direction, turning right out of the cobbled yard along the road was Whitedale Station, where we sometimes caught the train either to Hull or Hornsea. Along this road was a round house which I thought fascinating, but possibly rather difficult to furnish.

There used to be shooting parties in the season, often with guests staying, some of whom would bring personal maids, chauffeurs, or valets whose presence in the servants' hall was welcome.

When Sir Terence and Lady Faulkner visited, a batman used to accompany them, not always the same one. One, I remember, was most comical. One day her ladyship asked how he got such a high polish on Sir Terence's riding boots, to which he replied, 'Spit and elbow grease, my lady.' Not a quip to cause falling about: it was the way he said it.

Captain Bethell was joint master of the Holderness Hounds along with Major Hillas, for whom I worked some years later. The kennels were in Rise village, which consisted mostly of cottages for the estate workers and the hunt servants. They were huntsmen and whippers-in.

We girls sometimes visited the kennels, especially when there were puppies. When the puppies were weaned, some were boarded out to tenant farmers, usually in pairs.

During the summer the puppy walking took place on one of the lawns. On this occasion the puppies were brought by the people with whom they were boarded and were judged and paraded. It was a social occasion attended by all the local gentry and farmers and estate workers and indoor staff. The puppies then joined the pack to be trained for the coming season.

Another great event was the point-to-point. Staff and estate workers were able to attend and were given a lift in any cars that were going. I can also remember all of us going in a horse-drawn wagonette to a gymkhana at Beverley. The wagonette drew into an inn yard, where we all alighted. It was left there, and the horse stabled until we were ready to return in the early evening.

The school cricket match was a big occasion. Master Tony was at boarding school. The cricket team came to play a match against the Rise team which consisted of estate workers, the butler and Captain Bethell himself. The pitch was on a lawn in front of the dining room windows. Children from the boarding school, parents and nannies attended. A buffet tea was provided, including much ice cream! Matches were also played with neighbouring village teams throughout the season.

# 5
# Next to Nature

To a young girl reared in the busy port and industrial town of Hull, living on a country estate was sheer heaven. The house was set in a huge park surrounded by extensive woods. There was a large herd of fallow deer. I loved to walk in the park and woods when off duty. There was a large lake with an island in the middle where ornamental ducks swam. Webb, the gamekeeper, used to row across in a small boat to feed them. The park was often littered with antlers. I loved watching the deer in family groups.

I always kept my place. I never dared ask Webb to row me across to the island, although I longed to do so. Servants simply did not do such things, even when the family was away from home. Being caught by another servant—a possible sneak—might have meant dismissal, so I behaved myself. Sixteen-year-olds were capable of behaving in those days.

The staff were given their share of venison. It was such a treat that I never minded eating the flesh, even though I had known the animals 'personally'. We were next to nature. The deer and ducks were daily reminders of the beauty of creation. The lesson that Mother Nature had her own way of doing things was taught in the kitchen and park by the household's primitive freezing arrangements. Woe betide the domestic who forgot that ice melts! If she allowed a flood in the larder, her superiors would freeze her!

At one end of the lake was a grassy mound with a door leading into it, and the mound was fenced. Many years before my time it was the ice store. When the lake was frozen over in the winter, the ice was removed and stored in this ice house for use in the kitchen.

In 1930, there were still no fridges. Ice boxes were used, large wooden chests with heavy lids. Both box and lid were lead-lined. Hundredweight blocks of ice were bought from an ice store in Hull to be put in the boxes. At the top of each box, inside, was fitted a slatted wooden shelf on which to store perishable food. There was a large, shallow enamel dish underneath to catch the water as the ice thawed. It was the kitchen-maid's job to see that it did not overflow. How long a block of ice lasted obviously depended on the temperature, and the kitchen maid who allowed flooding got a reprimand.

Making ice cream in those days was quite a performance, but what delicious ice cream it was. There is no modern ice cream remotely like it. The ice cream machine was a large wooden tub with a cylindrical, galvanised container in the centre which revolved on a pivot. The ice cream mixture went into this, and the lid was clamped on. Chopped ice was packed around the cylinder, also salt to assist freezing. A handle was fastened on the lid and it was turned until the ice cream was made. The churning over, the handle was removed and more ice and salt packed round the sides and piled on top. Everything was covered with clean sacks to keep the cold in. It would keep like this for a considerable time.

Working for so many years in the country, I learned to love it in all its moods and seasons. I don't think I have a favourite season, each brings its own particular beauty. Even a bare tree against the winter sky is lovely, and how delightful the embroidery of hoar frost on twigs and branches. The commonest weed is transformed into something exquisite by frost.

Deer watching gave me joy at Rise Park. I never got close, timid as they are. The closest was when a young fawn basking the sun beside a fallen branch sprang from under my foot as I, unaware of the animal's presence, stepped over the branch.

I marvelled at their ability to hide themselves in the undergrowth and bracken. They came out from concealment to feed at dusk and dawn.

I loved the dappling of the fallow deer, and the attractive flattened shape of their antlers. These deer stand about three feet high at the shoulder, so when watching them in the park or wood even this five-foot-two admirer did not feel overwhelmed.

Deer chew their cud. They eat grass and herbs, but their vegetarian diet extends to young beech branches, and for kicks they will tackle the bark of a young fir. They like the resin. I am sorry they attack the beech, because I believe it is a non-conductor of lightning, and I hate lightning.

They can become a nuisance by making a meal of transplants and seedlings. 'I've either got to keep them off the young trees with a 6ft fence, or shoot a few,' Webb, the gamekeeper at Rise, told me.

Webb assured me that rabbits do far more harm than deer. They are particularly destructive to plantations of young trees, which even a small coney colony will exterminate.

Webb's defence against Bunny was fine-meshed wire netting a yard high with the lower 6in bent at right angles and pegged down.

I would sit quietly by the lake, where there was a wealth of wild life to be seen. A vole made an arrow head in the water with the tip of his nose as he swam. A mate of his might be sitting on a lump of clay, washing his face. Herons, drab and grey, were occasional visitors, but I preferred the brilliant blues and greens of the kingfishers and dragonflies.

House martins built under the eaves at Rise each year. There was a pair over our bedroom window, and we were able to admire their nest as a small miracle of architecture. In the course of construction many clay pills were dropped on the window-sill. No human builder can outdo this bird, with a small beak her only tool.

The woods at Rise were a sea of bluebells in the early summer, the azure mass speckled with the white stars of the wood anemone. Some of the rides were banked with rhododendrons, covered in blooms of glowing, jewel-like colours. Walking by these handsome bushes one day, the kitchen-maid and I saw three young weasels at play. Presently one stood on his hind legs sniffing the air. They had caught our scent and they were off into the undergrowth in a flash. Weasels are small and dun-coloured, and they live on rats and mice. Stoats, also rodent-eaters, are bigger—about 15in long—and chestnut brown and white, all white in winter in the north. Webb told me that southern stoats change their coats only partially, if at all.

But I think of high summer and the peace of the woods, broken only by the soft cooing of a pigeon or the startled cry of a pheasant at the sound of a snapped twig.

I knew where to find badger setts. Badgers had colonised the park before man arrived. Webb liked badgers, and he said they did practically no harm at all on the estate, except for one bad habit. Their powerful claws played havoc with his wire netting, especially if it went across their old runs.

Later on, at Thornhaugh, the second housemaid Florence and I walked the fields and woods together. Once we found the gamekeeper's gallows with various vermin hanging from it, a grisly sight. The predators, the stoats and weasels, were hanging there. They take the eggs and young of game birds. There were also two big rats and three grey squirrels, and a crow and two magpies shared their fate. The gruesome display was a warning and an advertisement of the gamekeeper's vigilance.

We housemaids picked wild lilies of the valley in woods where they grew in snowy drifts. We gathered cowslips for Hilda to make wine. Cowslips have other uses apart from wine-making. The flowers have freckles and that is why there is a countryside belief that cowslip water or ointment will remove freckles and sunburn. Hilda reminded me that children used to make cowslip balls, attaching clusters of flowers to a string stretched across two chairs, then drawing the flowers together into a golden globe. But what a waste of cowslips!

In the autumn we went mushrooming. In one field they grew in great white patches, some as big as dinner plates and they had a delicious flavour. But I did not fancy the horrid-looking fungus one of the French governesses I've known brought into the house. It was reluctantly cooked by Hilda, who told Mademoiselle she ate it at her own risk. She survived.

Mademoiselle saw the sloes Hilda was going to use for sloe gin. She made me laugh when she told me French children say you can't whistle after eating sloes. I am little inclined to believe superstitious fears about plants and certainly those concerning the flowers of the sloe, or blackthorn. The flowers appear before the leaves, and I believe that is why country folk are loathe to take the blossom into their houses, because of its apparently premature death.

While in service near Peterborough I was asked to go to the woods to pick primroses to sell in aid of the local hospital. Armed with a basket and a ball of wool for tying, we spent a pleasant afternoon bunching as we picked, with a circle of leaves around each bunch of flowers. They were sold at twopence a bunch.

What colour is the primrose? Webb maintained that it is sulphur-coloured, but artists and poets say it is a delicate green. Some primroses are almost white. What do you think?

What a lot we can learn from nature regarding colour harmony. The thought of purple with yellow makes me frown, yet those are the colours of the woody nightshade flower. Nature is a better colour schemer than Man.

Apart from love of the countryside, I learned a lot in my days of domestic service about dress sense and good manners, and I acquired an appreciation of quality furniture, china and pictures.

I also learned the value of dignity, and that is demonstrated by a true story told me by Jack, my husband.

One household he served had a donkey, an entire, but the children mistakenly called him Rachel when he was a foal! One of the young daughters took Rachel into the drawing room, where he promptly misbehaved. That donkey was no lady!

Madam rang for the butler and asked him to send a housemaid with dustpan and brush. When she arrived and saw the mess she said it was not her job to clean up donkey business, or words to that effect. Madam replied, 'I know that', and she took the dustpan and scooped up the mess.

She handed back the dustpan, saying, 'Would you mind taking this away for me, please?'

The child was scolded, and I hope the housemaid appreciated that personal dignity can be entire as well as donkeys.

# 6
# Sounds and Smells

Apart from clock chimes, there are certain sounds and smells which always bring back dear Rise to me. Wood pigeons cooing, the scent of hyacinths, to me a heavenly perfume, and Mrs Bethell's sitting room always seemed to have that fragrance about it.

Cucumbers take me back to the kitchen passage where the refreshing smell of them lingered. Half a century ago, but I am taken happily back.

I first saw budgerigars at Rise. There were three in a long cage in the sitting room window.

After I had spent about one year in this bit of heaven, a scullery maid was once more employed and I was upgraded to third housemaid. All day, and every day, I was with Alice and Emma! I then had the nurseries and the French Governess's room to do in addition to staff rooms. In the evenings I had to do my share of the mending of the household linen, as all housemaids do.

The change meant, to my delight, that I was able to see other rooms in the 'front' which hitherto had been out of bounds to me. You could live as a servant in the house for years without seeing even half of it! I could not explore when the family was away. I was as concerned about Alice's presence as that of the mistress. Once, when Alice had a half day, I sneaked around with Emma, but I was afraid to linger in any room. I have often thought how I would love to go back to Rise and wander again in the park and, most of all, through the house, of which I only ever saw that small part.

Unfortunately, I was unable to conquer my nervousness of Alice, and so I left and took a post as third housemaid at Middleton Hall in the Wolds.

Middleton Hall was considerably smaller. The Hellyers, who lived there, were very wealthy and of the merchant class. There were six indoor staff, a chauffeur and two gardeners.

The Hellyers had six children, but only one was at home. Enid, the youngest, was still in the nursery and was looked after by a nursery governess. The eldest son, Mark, was at Cambridge. The rest were at boarding school.

As nursery housemaid, my duties included cleaning the nursery wing, taking up the meals and washing the nursery dishes.

I went through a phase of breaking things. Did I have a ball! Every day, in spite of hoping that there would be no further casualties, the more I tried to be careful, the more objects were in danger.

Every Monday I turned out the night nursery. As we used brooms for all cleaning, considerable dust was created. So all ornaments, photographs and other things lying about were put on the bed and covered with a dust sheet. Pushing a chest of drawers along the floor to clean behind it, I knocked the knob off the door. I threw the knob on the bed and broke two ornaments. So I had three breakages to confess. The nursery governess, Miss Vaughan told me, with a grin, to stop playing pitch and toss!

The lighting in this house was by gas—not mains gas, but acetylene made on the premises. It produced a fan-shaped flame which we would now consider poor, but we managed to sew and knit quite well by it. Lighting up at night and winter mornings was quite a job. The housemaids had to go round every room with a taper. Some of the lights were hung from the ceiling by a brass chandelier. To reach these we had a long holder rather like a cigarette holder into which we secured the taper.

The Hellyers had a summer residence at Brixham, high up on the cliffs on the Berry Head Road, overlooking Tor Bay. My bedroom looked out across the bay to Torquay. The lights at night were very pretty. All the family and staff went there for the whole of the summer holidays, which was enjoyable. Brixham, in 1932, was a delightfully quiet fishing village.

Transport to and from Middleton Hall was poor, and spoiled days off. There was not the same degree of comfort as at Rise, and the food, though good and plentiful, was less appetising than that provided by Hilda. Perhaps I was prejudiced, but food varied from one house to another, depending on the cook. My sister was always as concerned over servants' hall food as she was with the dining room, so food wherever she was responsible was cooked to the same high standard.

I managed to stay one year at Middleton Hall but finally I found the frequent changes of staff rather unsettling. Mrs Hellyer did not want me to leave—in spite of my sessions of pitch and toss! All the time I was at Middleton Hall I neither spoke to Mr Hellyer nor saw him, except from a distance.

My next house was Thornhaugh Hall, a large house near Peterborough owned by Mr and Mrs Brotherhood. My sister was already working at Thornhaugh, so when an extra housemaid was needed she spoke for me. That's how I got the post. I was third housemaid at this modern house, built in 1926. Not modern enough to have wash basins in bedrooms, so we still had the carrying of hot water to the bedrooms in the usual brass cans, which had to be polished every day.

All the door knobs and finger plates on every door in the house both in the back and the front were brass to be kept polished. Each door had four plates, one above and one below the knob on each side of the door.

Hot water was taken to every bedroom in the front of the house four times a day. There were four in the family, including two grown-up daughters, and frequently there were visitors.

The butler took the gentlemen their water when calling them in the morning, and the ladies' maid 'watered' the two daughters and their mother when they were called. At lunchtime, dressing time in the evening and bedtime, housemaids took the water round.

If there was a hot water cosy, that was put over the can, like an outsize tea-cosy. If there wasn't one, then a hand towel was folded and placed over it. Then we had to go round all the rooms again after everyone had gone downstairs, and empty the washing water and clean out the handbasins. Every morning and evening bath mats had to be laid down in all bathrooms, and in each a bath sheet—a bath towel about two yards by one and a half yards—was laid on a chair ready for use.

When a personal maid was employed, the housemaids never touched the lady's dressing table. Her personal maid always dusted it and cleaned her toilet articles, brushes and mirror. The housemaids were otherwise responsible for the bedroom. All downstairs rooms were cleaned before breakfast.

Visiting ladies were always 'maided' by the housemaids, the usual rule being the head housemaid for the married ladies, the second housemaid for the single ladies, unless their own personal maid travelled with them. 'Maiding' meant seeing to all their needs while they were guests in the house. Their luggage was unpacked on arrival and packed ready for departure at the end of their visits. They would be called in the mornings at a time requested by them, with a tray of tea and biscuits or thin bread and butter, whichever they preferred.

Their day clothes were placed ready for them over a chair. Later, their evening clothes were put out. Underwear was placed on a chair and covered with a dress cover, which was usually a square of silk or other fine material. If they had no dress cover, then their dressing gowns would be placed over the garments and their slippers in front of the chair. Their evening dresses would be laid full length on the bed with the shoulders up on the pillows.

While the family and guests were having dinner, we housemaids did the tidying. We each had our allotted tasks. In this house with three housemaids, Annie, the head, straightened the newspapers and magazines and placed them neatly on a table set aside for this purpose. Florence, the second housemaid, shook up the cushions and emptied the ash trays; I, being third, swept the ashes into a pile under the grate, and folded the towels and cleaned the wash basin in the cloakroom.

We then went back upstairs, where we cleaned out any baths which had been used, emptied wash basins and tidied wash stands. The beds were then turned down, Annie and Florence doing the 'front' ones, and I did my sister's, as well as that of the ladies' maid.

Between these evening duties, we had all the household linen to repair, also the gentlemen's socks and underwear. The amount of mending varied. When the laundry came back, we had to open out every article—sheets, table cloths, pillow cases—to see what required mending. Nothing was ever put away without being mended. Sheets were turned sides to middle. If the sheet was thin down the middle, it was cut down the centre and the thinnest part taken out. Then the outer edges, being still sound, were seamed and the thin middle part, which now became the sides, was hemmed—and all this by hand!

Holes in pillow cases, towels, dinner napkins were darned with a flax thread; fine flax for linen, coarser for towels. When they were too worn to be darned, they were patched.

I got a bit homesick. I wrote home every two or three weeks. Mail for the whole house was delivered to the butler's pantry. The butler sorted it, taking the family mail to be set out on the front hall table, each person's mail in a separate pile. The servants' mail was set out in the same way on a table in the serving hall.

Unlike the formidable Alice at Rise, Annie, the head housemaid at Peterborough, was a quiet, gentle person, quaint and old-fashioned. I never saw her cross. She was plucky enough to go off alone every year for holidays abroad. Foreign holidays were not common in the 1930s.

Peterborough was our nearest town for shopping and cinemas. To catch the bus we had to walk to Wansford, a considerable distance, and on summer evenings back from there. In the winter a car was sent to meet us, as the lady of the house said she didn't like us walking on that lonely road in the dark, as we could be 'cut up in little pieces and no one would know.' I very much doubt if that would have happened in those peaceful law-abiding days. Now it certainly would not be safe.

Many of the big houses used to run a small sweepstake for the big horse races among the staff. Tickets were usually about 6d each and the kitty divided into first, second and third prizes. At Thornhaugh, the two young ladies of the family used to come to the servants' hall the night before a big race to draw the horses. All the staff used to assemble in the servants' hall for the draw. I won first prize with Golden Miller—£1—and thought that was marvellous wealth. My wages were only 10s a week at the time.

On Christmas Day a cold lunch was put in the dining room for the family and they helped themselves. The family had their Christmas dinner at night. The married estate workers were each given a cockerel from the home farm and a Christmas pudding.

The village children had a party in the village hall with everything provided by Mrs Brotherhood. There was a Christmas tree from which Father Christmas gave a present to each child after tea. The cakes, jellies and various treats were all made by my sister, which must have been a mammoth task. We all helped with sandwich making, laying of tables and serving the tea. This was followed by games for the children.

One year a ball was held in aid of the Peterborough hospital. A party of guests stayed for the occasion. The dividing screen in the front hall was pushed back and the double doors removed from the drawing room to make one big room for dancing.

There was a dinner party before the ball started for the guests who were staying at the hall. Just as dinner was about to be served, the billiards room chimney caught fire. What a panic there was! The room, intended for sitters-out, was full of smoke and lumps of red hot soot fell on the lawn outside.

The Brotherhoods' youngest daughter was married at St George's, Hanover Square, and coaches were hired to take all the staff and estate workers to London for the occasion. She would have preferred a wedding at the village church but her father was determined to have a big London wedding.

When we arrived, we all had lunch at Gunters' in Bond Street, then we went to St George's for the service, and later to the reception at her aunt's house in Rutland Gate, where all the presents were on show. The wedding presents were magnificent gifts of china, glass and silver. The bride was the pony club secretary and they gave her a life-size silver statue of a fox, which I admired enormously. There were three long trestle tables full of gifts.

Servants who went to the wedding service sang the hymns lustily. It was a long service, but all eyes were wide open and we enjoyed every moment. I wore my best dress and hat. We were allowed to eat with the guests. This was the only society wedding I ever attended.

Thornhaugh Hall burned down a year after I left. I used to think how dangerous it was. Cellars housed furnaces for heating. Logs were stacked near them, also discarded newspapers, dusters hanging to dry. Only a stray spark needed to send the whole place up, as it did!

# 7
# Isolation

Isolation. Sometimes living in a big country house meant that. This was fine for friends of Royalty who wanted to entertain their exalted visitors in private. It could be purgatory for the staff.

I was to enjoy close-ups of Royalty at Burwarton House in Shropshire, where I had my next post. Everything at that establishment—all linen, towels, sheets, china on the washstands, and chamberpots—bore the letter 'B' with a coronet.

'B' could well have stood for 'big'. The house was enormous. I went there as third housemaid of five. There was an indoor staff of twenty-two. The house had thirty-four bedrooms. As in all big houses, members of the staff were allowed only in the part of the house for which they were responsible, so, sadly, I never saw all over the house.

'B' was intended to stand for 'Boyne'. The estate was owned by Lord Boyne, whose wife was a sister of the late Earl of Harewood. Consequently, we used to have members of the Royal Family staying from time to time, especially the late Princess Mary with her two boys, the present Earl of Harewood and his brother.

When Royal visitors came, only senior staff was allowed to

serve them. I never came within yards of the King. There were three front staircases. Only one of them was ever used by Royalty. A second was for important visitors, the third for the family.

The house was silent. You could hear a pin drop. The deadly atmosphere was enlivened only by birdsong.

At the time I was there, there was neither a bus nor a train service. We used to be taken into Bridgnorth, which at that time was a very small market town. Half the staff went each Saturday afternoon; also any estate workers who wanted to go. We went in the shooting brake, driven by the under-chauffeur. We left the house at 2pm and returned at 4pm, so we went to town for two hours per fortnight!

The under-servants had to be in by 9pm, which was no hardship since there was nowhere to go. Under these conditions it was very difficult to keep staff. I did not stay long, but found it an interesting experience.

As in other establishments, most mealtimes passed in purgatorial silence. We longed to talk or laugh, but had to remain silent. I used to exchange sign language at Rise Park with Emma to make up for the monasterial quiet. If I raised an eyebrow it meant, 'Will you please pass me the marmalade?'. A twitch meant I fancied the cake nearest to her. At suppertime we were allowed to talk, and we had a fine time gossiping with visiting maids and chauffeurs.

We had to be up at 5am in the winter at Burwarton House when there were fire grates to clean, but 6am in the summer. Cleaning the grates was not my favourite occupation, and not just because of the loss of an hour in bed. I had the library and drawing room grates to clean. The library grate was made completely of brass except for the fire bars, which were steel, with a huge brass fender and fire irons. The drawing room grate was of steel with a huge steel canopy over it, steel fender and steel fire irons. All had to be polished daily. The surroundings were of white marble, all elaborately carved. The mantelpieces were about 8ft from the floor and were reached with steps. The head housemaid used to clean these two periodically with a mixture of soft soap and a very fine scouring powder made into a paste, which she called 'pickling' them. She would usually inform me that she was going to 'pickle' one of the fireplaces, after I had polished it, which meant it got splashed, so had to be polished again, and I dared not say anything about wasting my time and hard work!

It was the only house in which I worked where the front bathroom taps were of silver plate and cleaned with Goddard's plate powder and meths.

There were two lady's maids, one for Lady Boyne and a young one for Miss Rosemary Hamilton-Russell, the daughter of the house, and her friend, Miss Mary Windsor Clive, who shared lessons during term time. Miss Mary went home for holidays. The girls were taught by a French governess and during term were permitted to speak only French.

Routine was different from that at any other house in which I had worked. There were many to feed and at mealtimes we were distributed about the house. Feeding was a complicated operation. Housemaids had breakfast and tea in their own sitting room upstairs, served by the fifth housemaid. The kitchen staff and two still room maids had their meals in a small room leading off the kitchen and still room respectively. The idea was to keep an eye on whatever was cooking.

All the remaining staff had dinner in the servants' hall, served by the hall boy. The butler sat at the head of the table and the valet at the foot. There were always two meat dishes, a different one at each end of the table, such as a joint and a casserole. We were asked, in turn, which we would like, the housekeeper sitting on the right of the butler serving the vegetables. After the meat course, we all stood up while the 'housekeeper's room' filed out of the door, which was respectfully held open by the hall boy. That is to say the housekeeper, butler, valet and two lady's maids had pudding in the housekeeper's room. After their departure, our pudding was served by the head housemaid, who was then left in charge and we were allowed to talk!

Housemaids, footmen, hall boy and under-chauffeur had

supper in the servants' hall, served by the hall boy. The 'housekeeper's room' supper was served there by the second footman, and kitchen and still room staff had their meals in their own rooms. Meals at Burwarton approached in wonder the loaves-and-fishes miracle!

The two young ladies and governess had all meals served by the second footman in the schoolroom.

Opposite the butler's pantry was a large flower room, where two gardeners came to water the plants and change them, and the cut flowers, as required. One wall was lined from floor to ceiling with cupboards where all manner of vases were kept. Down the middle of the room was a long table, also a sink, and slippers into which the gardeners could change. Every morning, along with these duties, the butler entered in a book on the hall table the temperature, rainfall and wind. There were gauges in the grounds.

As in all houses, we tidied at lunchtime and dinnertime. Head housemaid, second, and myself tidied the drawing room, library and smoke room. The head folded newspapers and tidied magazines on a table kept for them. The second housemaid shook up cushions, and I swept up the fireplaces. The fourth housemaid tidied the study and Lady Boyne's sitting room, and the fifth housemaid looked after the cloakroom. As always, we walked everywhere in our correct order.

At this time the Boynes also had a house in Bedale for the grouse shooting, Brancepeth Castle in County Durham, and Belgrave House, where they went for the London season, in Belgrave Square. A small staff was kept at each of these houses and when the family were in residence, extra staff were taken from Burwarton.

The last I heard of the house was about 1965, when it was shown on television being used as a pony trekking hostel. No doubt only part would be used.

* * * *

There were good and bad servants, and the same applied to the jobs available to them. The bad places gave domestic service its poor image. I was lucky. I experienced only one really unsatisfactory situation. The isolation of Burwarton House was my sole reason for leaving there. Burrell Park was isolation plus. I soon found I had jumped from the frying pan into the fire when I took the post of under-housemaid.

In addition to the house being removed from the rest of the world, the servants' accommodation and food were poor, and the owner had a strange mental affliction which separated him from the household, so that he was virtually in solitary confinement.

Set in a large park, the house was magnificently built of white stone with an imposing pillared portico. The front door opened into a mahogany and glass porch. All the doors at the front of the house, both upstairs and down, were of mahogany with a broad, carved white-painted architrave. The skirting boards in every room were carved to a depth of 4in, with a further 8in of plain board below that. The whole of the skirting was painted white. Just imagine the work keeping all that clean!

The massive main door opened into a white marble paved hall about twenty-four feet square. To the right of the door was the principle staircase sweeping up in a grandiose curve, with wrought iron banisters topped by a broad mahogany hand rail. Opposite the front door were grand marble steps leading to a marble-paved corridor. All this spelt opulence with an astonished 'O', and I much admired the front of house even when once a fortnight I had to help the between-maid to scrub the vast expanse of floor. I admired the whole place, but I had no affection for it.

The first floor accommodation included two housemaids' sitting rooms. I never worked out why there were two. We used one on weekdays and the other on Sundays. I thought this arrangement both stupid and unnecessary, but there was much more that was stupid about Burrell Park.

The staff rooms were on the top floor and sparsely furnished. Underfoot in each room was cold lino, apart from a small bedside rug. The rooms had dormer windows, quite small and set so high that by standing on a chair I could just see over the windowsill. The manservants' rooms were along the same landing, but separated by a door which was locked, and kept permanently so by removal of the key!

'Sir Walter', the owner, had some years previously suffered a hunting accident resulting in brain damage. He seemed to have the mentality of a small child and was quite harmless. The poor man was segregated from the rest of the family. He had a bedroom on the front landing, and a sitting room on the back landing, where his meals were taken to him. Both rooms appeared to leave much to be desired, comfort-wise. In the time I was there I was never aware of the family communicating with him. I do not know whether or not he was able to speak, but I never heard him utter a sound. He seemed to spend his days gazing aimlessly out of the windows of whichever of the two rooms he happened to be in. On fine days, the butler, who had charge of him, took him for walks.

There was a staff of seven. Apart from me this consisted of cook, the kitchen-maid, who never came into the servants' hall to a meal, two housemaids, the butler and footman. The butler was Irish and, surprisingly, taciturn. The head housemaid was Scottish and from her I learned the meaning of the word 'dour'. The two of them having little to say, and the rule in most houses being that under-servants should be seen and not heard, most meals were taken in silence.

The servants' hall was a bare barrack-like room, the furniture consisting of a cupboard, a table and two wooden forms. The windows were big, without curtains. The staff's china, glass and cutlery were kept in the cupboard. The table, a long one, was in the centre of the room and the forms were the same length — just the setting for the musical 'Oliver', except that it was not 'food, glorious, food', and I don't suppose we would have got 'more'. Our staple diet was cold boiled bacon. We had other things at times, but that certainly predominated.

The family were Catholics. There was a chapel in the house

for their worship. The door into the gallery of the chapel was opposite the pantry. The family used the gallery and the village people the main body of the chapel, which was entered through a door in the back hall. One of the bedrooms was occupied at weekends by the priest. He came every Saturday evening in time for dinner. He took Mass on the Sunday morning, and left after lunch on that day. At least the priest and the villagers provided a change of faces.

The only other possible change was a brief sortie by private bus, lasting less than two hours on an afternoon off, to the nearest town 10 miles away.

There was no radio for the staff, and as there were no mobile libraries in those days, reading matter was in short supply. The young between-maid lived in the village and the two kitchen staff were in cycling distance of home, so they were able to escape on their days off, which no doubt made the place a little more bearable for them.

There is little wonder that I tolerated this 'prison' for only two months. It was dire misery after the comfort and happiness experienced in two of my previous places, especially Rise Park.

# 8
# The King's Friends

Next I went to Grove Lodge, Windsor, the home of Sir Colin and Lady Keppel. This house, I heard in 1951, was a girls' private school.

I was amused the day I arrived at Windsor. Instead of the usual chauffeur-driven car to meet me, Lady Keppel herself came—by bus! As the train drew in, there stood this frail-looking old lady on the platform. She enquired if I was for Grove Lodge. Then she called a porter for my luggage, and he put us on the bus in the station yard, her ladyship getting the tickets. Off we went, with Lady Keppel chatting to me and other passengers!

Sir Colin was a retired admiral who, for twenty years previously, had been Sergeant at Arms in the House of Commons. When the House was sitting, he stayed in a flat at the Palace of Westminster, going home only at weekends. As he could not drive, he travelled by train to Windsor, with a taxi to take him to Winkfield Row, the village in which Grove Lodge was situated. When he retired from the House, the Keppels did not go about very much, so no doubt thought a car and chauffeur quite unnecessary.

The Keppels were a great naval family, and the front stairs and landing were panelled with timber from one of the sailing ships in which Sir Colin's father had served. Also, on the front landing were models of sailing ships he had commanded.

An exquisite silver model of a sailing ship, complete with every detail of rigging, was the centrepiece of the dining table. Sir Colin himself sailed several times on the Royal Yacht.

The lighting here was again acetylene gas and they were running a fridge on it!

Beatrice, the kitchen-maid, and I shared a room and became great friends. It was here that I learned to ride a bicycle, giving poor Beatrice some shocks in the process. I cycled to Virginia Water to see Hilda, who by this time was married. Going through Ascot before coming to Fort Belvedere, the then Prince of Wales's residence, there is a very steep hill, known as Wells Hill. I was determined to ride up it. There were some men working on the road. Seeing me pedalling wearily up, they started to sing, 'Oh, I Love to Climb the Mountains', a popular song of the day. I had to get off and walk as I could no longer cycle for laughing.

Lady Keppel organised a sewing and knitting party known as Queen Mary's Sewing Guild. The village women assembled with her ladyship every Monday afternoon in the dining room to make garments for the poor people of London's East End.

It was quite a business. The work was kept in tea chests in a spare staff room; also a box of toys for any children who came with their mothers. These were carried down by the footman as soon as lunch had been cleared away.

The dining chair seats were upholstered in velvet, so she had some cotton covers made which I had to tie over the seats with tapes to prevent sticky fingers marking them. Mrs Stacey, the cook, made a huge batch of rock cakes; tea and cakes were served during the afternoon.

Usually the bell rang several times during the afternoon to announce 'Mrs Smith's little Johnnie would like some lemonade', home-made of course. Or 'Mrs Jones's Mary would rather have milk!' So the footman, Arthur, was kept going pretty well for most of the afternoon. When all had departed, I then had to remove the covers, sweep up the crumbs, squashed currants and other debris from the carpet. I don't know how many garments were produced at these sessions. Lady Keppel spent most of her time crocheting squares and making them into attractive blankets.

I remember one evening Lady Keppel going down to dinner wearing nail polish. Sir Colin asked what was on her fingers. When she replied 'Nail polish, dear,' he told her 'Get it off. You look like a harlot!'

The Keppels were personal friends of King George V, for whom Sir Colin was, at one time, an equerry. At Christmas they were guests of the Royal Family at Sandringham. After spending a week there, they went on to Quidenham Hall in Norfolk to stay with the Earl of Albermarle, Sir Colin's brother.

George Higgs, the butler, went with them to valet Sir Colin, as did Jean, the head housemaid, to maid her ladyship as she did not have a lady's maid. George and Jean enjoyed Sandringham and the gifts they received from the royal Christmas tree. Presents for each member of the staff and visiting staff were handed from the tree by the Prince of Wales, later the Duke of Windsor.

A house in Chester Square was rented for the London season. As the Keppels hadn't a town house, this was done every year and for many years the same char used to do the rough work throughout the stay.

King George V died the night before we went up to town so, of course, with the court in mourning, there was no season, but as the house had been rented for that period, we stayed.

I remember everyone listening to each bulletin on the radio and Mrs Stacey crying when the King's death was announced. The housekeeper and butler had been huddled over the radio. The other servants listened outside the door, as they had no radio of their own.

To me the King was a remote figure. But I felt very differently when I heard of King George VI's death. I was quite stunned and felt real sadness for the Queen Mother and our Queen, especially the Queen, having to take on the great task so young. I am furious when anyone dares to criticise her, be it a Member of Parliament or anyone else.

Sir Colin, being a close friend of the late king, attended the funeral in spite of being well over seventy (I think he was about seventy-six). He insisted on donning his Admiral's uniform and following the cortège on foot. When the procession reached Hyde Park Corner, he collapsed and was brought back to Chester Square in a taxi. He was confined to bed for several weeks and was unable to leave the house for the remainder of our stay.

Upstairs and downstairs! This was my first experience of a London house, and I found it very different from country houses. It seemed very strange having the drawing room on the first floor. Arthur's room was in the basement next door to the butler's pantry, as were the servants' hall and kitchen. George's room was on the ground floor at the top of the basement stairs. We girls had our rooms at the top of the house on the third floor. They were much smaller than at Grove Lodge, with bars at the windows and very hot. The whole house seemed very cramped, even impoverished! I think we were all very pleased to return to Grove Lodge at the end of the season.

So ended my first taste of 'upstairs and downstairs'. I much preferred country houses. London houses seemed dull and cramped after sprawling, mellow country establishments. And I hated the staff's claustrophobic bedrooms!

Some time after we returned to Grove Lodge, Sir Colin received from Queen Mary the late king's tobacco jar from Sandringham and a paper knife from his desk on the Royal Yacht. Sir Colin also received a cup of sorrow, of which there were only a limited number made, being commissioned by Queen Mary. It was a large goblet with both the heads of Queen Mary and King Edward VIII engraved on it, with an inscription. They would no doubt be of great value today, as would the collection of bronzes at Grove Lodge. There were about twenty bronzes of various sizes—animals, birds, gargoyles and Chinese gods. They were on a long shelf, and they were the bane of my life. They were in the front hall, which I had to clean every morning, and dusting them was, to say the least, time-consuming.

Shortly after our return to Grove Lodge we had a change of butler. The butler who took George's place was the effeminate one. There was a great array of Roger & Gallet creams on his dressing table. One evening, when he was serving dinner, Sir Colin asked him if he had perfume on, to which he replied it was Arthur the footman's hair cream!

About this time Beatrice left to get married. We had been good friends and I had grown fond of her, so I missed her very much. The girl who took her place was a rather rough type. I could not take to her at all and found sharing a room with her uncomfortable, so I decided to leave.

* * * *

In spite of my passion for the truly rural, I was about to take a post in town. There was a vital reason for this, which I shall later disclose.

I had worked in pretty surroundings. From my bedroom at Thornhaugh I could see the grounds, which were delightfully laid out. I looked across the circular front drive with its pair of tall wrought iron gates. The drive's terraced lawn had two long lily ponds with fountains. The lawn was surrounded on three sides by a wood. From the far end of the lawn was a ride through the wood to fields beyond and, in the distance, Wittering Church. It really was a picture postcard view, and on a fine warm night I loved to sit at my window to enjoy the vista of fountains and woods dripping with moonlight. It would have made a lovely setting for a romantic film.

Cinemas in those days were dream palaces in which to forget the facts of hard life, where the golden lads and lasses of the screen lived in surroundings as stately as those I was accustomed to as a domestic servant. In those pre-television times I was fond of the movies myself. My top male favourites were Leslie Howard, Herbert Marshall and George Sanders. I also liked Rex Harrison, who was much nicer then than he was later on! Janet Gaynor, Joan Crawford, Maureen O'Sullivan, Greta Garbo and Bette Davis were among the actresses I enjoyed seeing.

Back to my window and the moonlight, lovely and ethereal. Moonlight—and masses of the estate's roses. What a setting for young love! Inevitably, there was the occasional staff romance, but it had to be handled with great discretion, for if the state of things became known it could mean dismissal for one, if not both, parties concerned.

Once, when I had been to the pictures with Hilda, we returned to the house to be confronted with a scene as exciting as anything we had seen in a film. There had been a burglary. The police were taking finger prints and we were told to search our belongings and report if anything was missing. The next day all who had been in the house at the time of the unpleasant occurrence were questioned. By that evening it became obvious who the burglar was, and a staff romance came to a sad ending.

A young footman, William, who was a nice, quiet lad became very fond of Grace, the second housemaid. No doubt she flirted with him, but his feelings for her were more than just that. She took up with a young man in the village called Cyril. Poor William became so incensed with jealousy that he decided, I suppose, to get his own back for the unhappiness this caused him, and stole a wrist watch given to her by Cyril.

He staged a burglary. One evening, when there were only a few staff on duty, and little chance of being caught in the act, he went to her room and took the watch. Grace went to turn down the beds in the staff quarters and was shocked to find one room ransacked, and her own room, next door, locked on the inside.

She rushed downstairs to tell William, who was washing glasses and silver in the butler's pantry. With a great pretence of concern, he went upstairs. By looking out of the window of the adjoining room, he could see Grace's window wide open. To the accompaniment of her pleas to be careful, he climbed out of the neighbouring window and went gingerly along a ledge and into Grace's room which was in even greater disorder than next door. He unlocked the door, went downstairs and, as the butler was off duty, told the master there had been a burglary.

A plaster cast was made of a footprint in the wet earth of the shrubbery and it fitted William's muddy shoes in his bedroom. After taking the watch he had jumped out of Grace's window on to the flat roof of a passage leading to the servants' hall and then down to the shrubbery. The last I saw of poor William was when he was taken away by the police.

Another staff romance which ended unhappily was mine! My friendship with their butler was the main reason for my leaving the Keppels. Nothing was stolen in our case unless it was my affection, which George eventually decided he could not return—not fully, anyway. But that was later.

When George Higgs and I were going out together we had to be very discreet. We used to meet away from Grove Lodge and on our return from an outing I usually went in first while he had a drink in the village, arriving back at the house later.

Our half days were spent walking in the Great Park, and once we walked to Eton to see the college. In the evening we indulged in my passion, the pictures.

Sundays were spent either at Virginia Water or visiting his widowed mother and younger sister at Yateley, near Camberley. His mother had a gold brooch which greatly intrigued me. It was a miniature of a pick and shovel, a souvenir of South African gold-mining. Her husband was valet to Cecil Rhodes, and he went to Africa with him.

George decided to leave Grove Lodge since keeping our friendship a secret was rather a strain. He took a butler's post in Eaton Square.

So I began to travel to London each half day to meet George there. I had my eye on that flat over the garage in Eaton Place Mews. This had always been occupied by the married butler in the past. We hoped, one day, to be the new tenants. I remember looking over it one afternoon, full of plans for the future, but it was not to be.

# 9
# Service Twosomes

I did not marry a butler, and I never wanted to be a cook. I could not have dealt with the blood and guts, though perhaps cake and pastry-making in the still room might have suited me.

How would my life have differed if I had married my butler friend? Or supposing I had been a footman's wife?

My sister Hilda and her husband Victor (privately Mr and Mrs Makins) served together as butler and cook at the home of Colonel Lloyd in Leicestershire.

Victor had started in service as a young boy five years before me in 1925. By the time I began, the gentry were closing many of their rooms and cutting down, as at Rise. I went in at the tail end of the great days and World War II finished it all.

Victor's first job was as door boy. His uniform was royal blue, the short tunic a 'bum freezer' with gilt buttons all down the front, and he wore white cotton gloves.

One of his duties was to be in the front hall to open and close the door when anyone entered or went out. The butler and first footman were also there. He did washing up, and had to go round lighting all the gas lights in the servants' hall, pantry and back corridors. It was acetylene gas, manufactured on the premises.

His next post was second footman of two. He advanced to

going into the dining room at lunch and dinner, at first just to carry in trays of food and take away the used dishes. The family were his guinea pigs when he trained to serve at table. He practised serving when only they were dining, so that he would know his duties at a lunch or dinner party when all hands would be required.

His next post was 'equal first footman'. He was the mobile one of the pair. He was carriage footman whenever the lady went out in the car. The chauffeur never left his seat behind the wheel. If the lady was calling and leaving visiting cards, Victor had to open the car door, help her out and ring the door bell. When she had made the call, he opened the car door, settled her back aboard, and closed the door. The next call might be a shop, a house for afternoon tea, or a bridge party. At times he was out all afternoon, hence the need for two first footmen.

After a dinner party the first footman and sometimes the butler had to stay on duty until the last guest had gone home (this was so in my day). There was usually a servants' hall full of chauffeurs, so plenty of talk going on. There were long dreary nights when the family or some member of the family was out at a dinner party, and he had to sit up until 3 or 4am to let them in. Likewise the lady's maid would have to sit up to put her lady to bed. And they had to be up at the usual time the next morning to start the day's work.

As well as pressing the daily paper with a warm iron, the footman had to damp and press the laces for the gentleman's evening dress shoes. Near the pantry was the brush room, where suits were brushed and pressed each time they were worn.

The footman had to clean the silver, being careful not to rub away the hall marks. The silver in everyday use was kept in the pantry in a cupboard which had a steel, safe-type door faced with wood to disguise its purpose. The main silver was kept in a strong room or large built-in safe in a room off the pantry. This was often the first footman's bedroom, with a bed which folded into the wall. In one house he had a 'let down' bed which came across the safe door.

The disguised silver cupboard reminds me of Lady Boyne's camouflaged jewel safe. There was an ordinary-looking tallboy outside his lordship's bedroom, with polished wood exterior. Behind the wooden door was the steel door of the safe.

Most butlers were married and had a cottage on the estate, but there was also a room for the butler in the house for late-night dinner parties. This was also the room he used when he changed for lunch or dinner.

At one house where Victor worked the lady and gentleman celebrated their golden wedding. To mark the occasion they found some fascinating old livery for the staff. Victor had a velvet jacket and breeches, with silver buttons on the jacket and silver buckles on his black shoes.

Whatever a footman's real name was, he was always given a 'standard' first name. The first footman was always James, the second was John and the third Charles. As it happened Charles was Victor's real second name so he was called by his actual name when he held the appropriate post.

There was an unbreakable rule for all menservants, hear nothing, see nothing, and above all, say nothing.

Victor recalls that on the forms sent from domestic agencies it was stated that if a servant left a post within the month another post would be found without a further fee being charged. Some places were so bad that a quick change had to be made. It was Victor who prompted me to admit that I worked briefly in a house, Burrell Park, where the conditions were quite awful. It was my original intention not to mention it.

* * * *

George and I had some very happy times in London. It was my first experience of the big city. Remember, as a domestic I was very much a country girl! We toured the usual places of interest, then had tea at a Lyons restaurant.

The smaller Lyons restaurants were staffed with Nippies, as the waitresses were called. The teashop waitress was something of a Cinderella and Lyons set out to improve her image.

'Nippy' suggested somebody sharp and prompt. I remember comparing the uniform with my own. Nippy wore a white mitre cap, a Peter Pan collar, soft turned-up cuffs, and a nippy little apron. The black buttons of her black corsage were sewn on with red thread, and she wore a medallion of office. Her skirt was just below the knee, and she wore black stockings and neat shoes. Very smart!

The Lyons in Piccadilly where we had tea was a big restaurant staffed not by Nippies, but by waiters. On the ground floor was a stage where there was an afternoon cabaret, so we took a table on the first floor, near the balustrade, which formed a well, where we could look down on the stage.

After tea we went to the Victoria Palace, where we saw two main films, news. and a variety show, all for 3s 6d each in the front circle! The evening was rounded off with coffee and biscuits at the Elephant and Castle snack bar at Victoria. I really thought I was living it up!

Beatrice had left Grove Lodge, and had been replaced by a ruffian, but more important, George had left. It was to be near him that I decided to take a post in town.

Sir Morton and Lady Smart were requiring a housemaid at their Grosvenor Square flat, and I arranged to go to them. They were on holiday in Jamaica, and did not require me until they returned. The family George was working for was going up to Scotland for the grouse shooting, taking all the staff. So as George and I would be apart for that time, I had to find a temporary job until the Smarts returned. I went with the Wilson shooting syndicate to Eggleston Hall, near Barnard Castle.

The Wilsons were of Tranby Croft, near Hull, a house where King Edward VII, when Prince of Wales, was a frequent visitor. The well-known Baccarat episode took place there. Stanley Wilson had a large house at Wimbledon. I stayed at the Wimbledon house one night so that I could travel up to Co Durham with the staff the following morning. Mrs Wilson stayed at Wimbledon. The syndicate consisted of Mr Stanley Wilson, Mr Arthur Wilson from Tranby Croft, Mr Wilson-Filmer, and the Earl of Munster. Mrs Wilson-Filmer and the

Countess of Munster, who was Mr Stanley's daughter, acted as hostesses.

The Countess of Munster was a concert pianist and had her grand piano taken to Eggleston Hall with her. I was interested when listening to a musical programme on the radio to hear that one of the pianists had received the Countess of Munster Award.

The butler, valet, second footman, hall boy, chauffeur, cook, head kitchen-maid and head housemaid from Wimbledon went with us. I, the third housemaid and the scullery-maid were all temporary workers for the season. Mrs Wilson had a small number of the permanent staff left with her at Wimbledon.

The Countess had her personal maid with her, as did Mrs Wilson-Filmer, whose maid was a Swiss girl, Mademoiselle Kerswetter, quite the nicest lady's maid I ever met. Most of them were inclined to be a little 'snooty' and at times condescending. Mademoiselle was always pleasant and full of fun. On several occasions, she sneaked across the yard to the men's wing to make 'apple pie beds' or tack up the ends of their pyjamas sleeves and trousers or, as they were folded under the top pillows, stitch them to the bottom one!

The staff went up to Eggleston to prepare the house one week before the syndicate arrived on 11 August ready for the first shoot on the 'glorious twelfth'.

In one wing of the house upstairs was a long corridor with several bedrooms and two bathrooms. At the end was a door, which we thought admitted either to a bedroom or a bathroom. We were surprised to find a large swimming pool. One of the best features of the house was the attractive front staircase which divided into two half way up.

We had a house party every week. Guests arrived in time for dinner Sunday evening and departed after breakfast the following Sunday. So the housemaids had a busy day, changing beds and preparing rooms for the newcomers.

Most of the guests brought a servant with them, some brought two. There were valets, lady's maids, chauffeurs, loaders, so at times we were quite a big party in the servants' hall. This was one house where there was no protocol. We were just one happy crowd. There always seemed to be plenty of conversation and laughter. We were very busy, but I enjoyed my two months' stay.

The third housemaid's father was the head gardener. Mary was an only child and they lived in the lodge at the main gate. It became a second home to me. Mary did the most exquisite fine crochet lace. She made a long table runner with swans and lily pools worked into it, a really lovely piece of work. The surrounding country was glorious, and Mary knew all the loveliest walks. I have always enjoyed walking, especially if the country is wild, such as moorland. A very good trout stream ran through the grounds, where Mr Stanley sometimes fished.

Again I encountered authority without the Alice touch. Kitty, the head housemaid, who had worked for the Wilsons previously, but returned temporarily, was a Scots girl from Caithness. She was small, slim, most attractive and very sweet and gentle. Mary and I liked her very much, and we pooled tips as a trio.

There was a big shoot from the house every day, with lunch taken up on the moors. This was the only time I knew of a shooting accident. One of the beaters got some pellets in his scalp. Luckily, as he was wearing a tweed deerstalker, they went only just below the skin. A doctor was called and the pellets removed. I don't think he was any the worse, apart from soreness. A good thing, perhaps, that the injury was not to the other end of him!

During our stay at Eggleston Hall the whole syndicate went away for a week to Doncaster races for the St Leger. Mr Wilson came to the servants' hall and told us to do as little work as possible and make it a holiday. So I enjoyed more walks! Six of us bought three 10s LNER 'runabout' tickets between us permitting journeys anywhere within a radius of 50 miles for the week.

My happiness was clouded about two weeks before the end of the season. I had, of course, written regularly to George in

Scotland and always looked forward to his letters. Alas, one morning I received a letter saying he wished to end our relationship. This was shattering news, as we had intended getting engaged on our return to London, and had made so many plans for the future.

I wanted to run away and hide. I soaked his letters in tears, and was very miserable, sniffing as I got through my work. I wanted to run to Hilda for sympathy. Reason for the break? He had found someone else, which is perhaps just as well, since he was a good deal older than me. Naturally, I did not think like that at this sorrowful time!

At the end of the season all the guests and syndicate departed. We were left for a week to clean through the house in readiness for handing over to the owner of the estate, who at that time was Sir William Gray. So we all went our various ways.

I was not due to take up my post with Lady Smart for another week. In spite of the break in our relationship, George's mother invited me to stay with her and her daughter. She was very kind to me and unhappy over what had happened.

# 10
# Town and Country

Then I went to Grosvenor Square. How very different from my previous experience of London, where George and I had such happy times. This time I hadn't even my dear friend, Beatrice. I found London a lonely place. I didn't know any one.

After I had been there a few months, I heard from Kitty, my new friend from Eggleston, that she was taking, as it were, a caretaker's post in the Charles Street house of Mrs Rupert Ward, sister of Mr Wilson. She had a house in Maryland and was visiting it for a few months, and asked Kitty if she would stay with two maids she was leaving there.

So, for a short time, I was able to visit Kitty and on one occasion met my Swiss friend again. The girls were on board wages, which was quite a usual thing when a family went away leaving staff behind. This meant each member of staff was given a set amount to live on in addition to the normal wage. In a happy household where everyone got on well together, one senior member would do the catering, each contributing a set sum each week. If she were a good manager the staff could find themselves a few shillings better off.

Alas, Kitty's term of employment in Charles Street came to an end. Girls who had a home to go to between jobs often did temporary work as a higher wage and all expenses were paid to temporaries. They had not quite the same responsibilities as permanent staff either; providing they did the work required of them, that was all that was expected.

Sir Morton Smart was manipulative surgeon to the Royal Family. Many notable people were among his patients, including foreign Royals. So we always had to be on our toes when answering the telephone or front door bell. Apart from members of our own Royal Family and foreign Royals being patients, they were also personal friends and were likely to call at any time.

A strict rule at Sir Morton Smart's was that we never gave information concerning his whereabouts unless the caller's name was acceptable, and we were instructed never to disturb him at weekends at his country address unless the inquirer was one of the royals.

One Sunday morning I answered the telephone to the film actor Tullio Carminati. I was thrilled, because *One Night of Love,* in which he appeared with the American operatic singer Grace Moore, was one of my favourite film musicals. Carminati was not a royal, but he was a count—Count Tullio Carminati de Brambilla.

I was very apologetic, and promised to pass the message to the butler at Bere. The Italian romantic actor arrived for a consultation a few days later and I made sure I got a good look at him!

The royals being personal friends as well as patients and liable to call in person or telephone at any time, we always had to be on our guard when answering the telephone or door.

Lady Smart was once nearly caught with her hair-do in disarray when a member of the Royal Family paid a personal call. She had long, corn-coloured hair which she wore in a plait around her head to frame her natural wave. One day, after shampooing her hair she had used extra pins to hold it until dry. She was in the sitting room when the Duchess of Kent was announced, and she had hurriedly to remove pins which I found stuffed down the side of an armchair the following day!

The Duchess apologised for calling at an inconvenient time. Did she notice the state of Lady Smart's goldilocks?

Another regular royal visitor was Queen Maud of Norway.

Sir Morton had served in the Navy for many years as a surgeon. When he retired Ranstead, his servant during his naval service, became his butler.

One day Ranstead had to go out on an errand and asked me to answer the telephone and door should anyone call. The telephone did ring. Someone wanted to make an appointment so I entered the name in the appointment book, 'Maud' Howland.

On the day this patient came, Ranstead opened the door to find Lord Howland standing there! He is now, of course, the Duke of Bedford.

While I was at Sir Morton's he started the London Clinic for Injuries on the corner of Grosvenor Square and North Audley Street. Queen Mary opened it for him, and I had a real close-up view of her. I was outside to see her arrive, and since it was a private opening—no neck-craning!

Sir Morton and Lady Smart were invited to attend the coronation of King George VI and Queen Elizabeth, now the Queen Mother.

Marjory, the housemaid whose place I had taken had left to get married to the head porter at a block of flats at 140 Park Lane. I had become friendly with her and, as we were going down to the country house the day after the coronation, I called to see her a few days before. To my delight Marjory asked me if I would like to see the procession. Her husband had been given tickets to view from a third-floor flat that was empty.

The night before Coronation Day, Kitty and another of her friends and myself went out to see the decorations. I got back to my room about 1am, but there was so much noise going on outside, as the streets were crowded all night, it was impossible to sleep. I had to call her ladyship at 4am anyway, and decided I might as well stay up and do my packing. So I never slept at all.

I remember her ladyship in long white gown and feathers. I wanted to tell her how nice she looked, but daren't. All the guests had to be in the Abbey by 6am and were not allowed out again for any reason until after the ceremony. They took a box of Horlicks tablets to sustain them through the day, and arrived home about 6pm. Then they changed and went to dinner with friends at Claridges.

The following day we drove down to Hampshire, to Bere Mill, their weekend retreat. It was a colourful drive with decorations in towns and villages all along the way.

The house was built on a plot of land which formed a peninsula in the Test, a river noted for salmon trout. The last I heard of Bere Mill was that it had been taken by a fishing syndicate, an account of which I read in the *Field.*

It was a delightful old place, surrounded as it was on three sides by the river, so that the gardens were split into three portions, connected by small bridges. At the back of the old mill adjoining the house was the huge water wheel still in perfect condition. I was told that at this mill the first paper money was made.

Sir Morton was a keen and very successful fisherman, and we enjoyed his catches. He also kept several of the village folk supplied with salmon trout. The Smarts frequently had friends to stay for a fishing weekend. One very interesting visitor was Mrs Pocock (Ruby M. Ayres, the novelist).

Another of Sir Morton's hobbies was growing gladioli, which he used to show at the International Exhibition at the Albert Hall, to which blooms were flown from all over the world. He won the cup on several occasions. He himself gave a silver cup for the best gladioli at the local produce show at Whitchurch.

Although a full-time gardener was employed, he was never allowed to touch the 'gladdies'. Sir Morton himself planted and looked after them. As the day of the exhibition drew near, an anxious watch was kept for signs of rain. He had some long paper bags made and, at the first sign of rain, we all rushed out and helped put a bag over each bloom. He also had long cardboard boxes made just wide enough to take two blooms placed at opposite ends. On the morning of the show, the car was loaded with the boxes, inside, in the boot and even piled on the roof.

He bred a very pretty gladiolus, a delicate pink, with smokey blue streaks. He named it Lady Morton, after his wife, but although I have searched bulb catalogues, I have never seen it and can't think why not, as it was most attractive.

The Smarts had many friends in Jamaica, where Sir Morton had for some years prior to his marriage served in a government post. When they went there for two months, I was given the choice of staying at Grosvenor Square or spending that time a Bere Mill. I had spent a very pleasant week there at Christmas and, as London was at that time a lonely place for me, I chose Bere Mill.

It was a very enjoyable time, a really delightful place to be in the summer. One day we were bathing in the river, as we did most afternoons, when we heard the garden gate close and footsteps on the drive. Peeping cautiously over the bank we were surprised and shocked to see the Duke and Duchess of Gloucester. We made a hasty retreat round the back of the mill, where a gardener was working, to ask him if he would tell them that Sir Morton and her ladyship were away from home!

The house was about one mile out of Whitchurch. Along the road was a disused quarry with a steep bank along the top of which was a footpath. The sides of the bank after dark were covered with glow-worms. One night I picked one up and even in my hand it glowed . . .

There were two pet birds; a green parrot called Nicky, a great talker, and a sulphur-crested cockatoo. During the summer we used to put Nicky on a perch in the garden, and he had great games with the postman and any tradesmen who called. He would wait until they were half way down to the gate, then call them back. Thinking it was someone from the house calling, they would come back to see what was wanted. He could laugh, cry, sing to order, and had a great fondness for calling to the postman, 'Come over here'.

He always slept in her ladyship's room and it was my job to carry him up at night and down in the morning. Mostly he would 'ride' quite happily on my finger but if he was feeling a bit out of temper would peck fiercely at my hand. Then I would have to get the small carrying perch. Through the day he lived in the kitchen on a large perch. If Kate, the cook, was chopping food at the table, he would keep up an incessant 'bit for Nicky!' The butler, against Sir Morton's advice, taught him to take pieces of food from his mouth, for which foolhardiness he paid with a torn lip.

The cockatoo lived in a big cage in the kitchen. She couldn't talk, only screech in an ear-splitting manner. Kate used to wedge a small hand brush between the cage bars, which petrified her into silence. A most cruel way of quietening her when a cloth over the cage would have had the same result and have been kinder.

Sir Morton would take her out of the cage for a period each day and Cocky would perch on his shoulder, whether sitting in the house or walking in the garden. During one of his garden walks, she was startled by something and flew up into a tree. What panic until a gardener managed to retrieve her.

* * * *

The most privileged pets in my stately homes were dogs. They roamed the house and were treasured members of the family. The staff liked them with reservations. They made extra work for the servants when shedding hair, and the staff were pleased when puppies were properly house-trained.

Cats and dogs! When I think of the animals I have known in the houses where I have worked, it's raining them. These creatures brought me a lot of pleasure and sometimes sadness. The Bethells had only two house dogs, and just one when Bingo, a golden and white 'Shelty' was killed instantly while dancing round the horses' feet when they were exercising. Captain Bethell at one time had fourteen hunters. One of them gave Bingo the fatal kick.

At Thornhaugh Mrs Brotherhood had a peke called No Nose. The two daughters had hounds as pets, one 'Elk', the other 'Irish Wolf'. When the beds were turned down at night, Florence the second housemaid had to put the dogs' beds ready, and spread out their blankets!

# 11
# Flora and Fauna

Etton Hall, near Beverley, was best for animals—and for flowers, and my post there proved to be the easiest job I ever had!

As I had not seen my father and two brothers for some years, I decided to apply for a post near my native town. I took a post as upper housemaid of two.

We were a staff of five looking after one gentleman, Major Newland Hillas, who was away far more than he was at home. He was joint master of the Holderness Hunt with Captain Bethell, my first country house employer. By a strange coincidence (for me) the hounds had been moved to Etton from Rise, and one of the Rise whippers-in had become the huntsman.

On the oak-panelled walls of the smoking room were several foxes' masks and brushes, as reminders of the major's function as joint master of the hunt. There was also a rug made from the skin of a fox hound.

He was a racing man as well as being MFH and had several racehorses, which were kept at the home farm, about a quarter of a mile down the road. The trainer lived in the farmhouse and there were several bothies for the jockeys and stable lads. Bothies were buildings where they lived as they were all single men. The trainer's wife used to cook for them. She also made all the butter for the house and dressed any poultry required.

There were two hunters: Whitwell, a bay, and a huge black horse, Jack. Sometimes, when the groom returned from exercising the horses, he put the reins over Jack's back after dismounting and Jack walked across to the kitchen door to bump it. Then the cook came out with some sugar lumps for him. This only happened if the Major was away from home.

One day we were having our 'elevenses' in the servants' hall when there was a clump, clump, up the passage. When I opened the door to see what was happening, there was Jack, with the groom grinning in the background.

An old hunter called Baby was pensioned off and through the winter lived down at the racing stables. In the summer she lived in a small paddock behind the tennis courts. There was an open shed where she could shelter if it rained. Whitwell and Jack sometimes joined her. By the gate into the paddock was a large tree under which she spent a lot of her time. From there she could see across the lawns to the house. She died just before the war. Two of the farm men and the groom and one gardener buried her beneath that tree and a brass plate was later fixed to it inscribed with her name and age.

Major Hillas had a motley crowd of dogs which he used to take out every morning when he went riding before breakfast. Rajah, the great dane, Peter and Sandy, the two labradors, three mongrel terriers, Warrior, Wilfred and Jill, lived in loose boxes in the stable yard and were fed and looked after by the groom.

They made an extraordinary sight when they followed the Major on his constitutional, a canine 'Uncle Tom Cobley and all'! Wilfred was a demon. If he got into the house and the dining or drawing room door was open, he would be in like a flash to cock his leg up at the velvet curtains.

Sandy was the Major's gun dog. Peter, who was nearly blind, was retired, but had been a gun dog. In the summer meat was bought from the butcher for them, but during the winter rabbits and hares were cooked for them in the saddle room by the groom.

In addition to these were three house dogs, and Wendy and

Mick, two Jack Russells which lived in the front of the house. Wendy went everywhere with the Major until she became too old to travel.

Once, when staying at Brown's Hotel in London, he ordered a chicken fricassee for Wendy. When the waiter brought it in a silver entrée dish, the Major put it down on the floor for her.

Valour, a rough-haired terrier, was my special favourite. He lived mostly in the servants' hall and was fed there and slept in my bedroom. I adopted him or he me, I'm not sure which. This was the nearest I had been to having 'my own dog'.

As in most houses, there was a baize-covered swing door from the front to the back of the house. Valour discovered that, if he took a running jump at it, he could nip through before it swung shut.

When I happened to go through to the front with my hands full, I used to push the swing door with my rear and nip through. Old Faithfull, the butler, on the other hand, always stood on one foot and pushed the door with the other. One evening while doing a little washing up in the butler's pantry, as I did sometimes to help the old chap, I heard a crash followed by a stream of oaths. When I went to investigate, there he was sitting in the middle of the hall rug, surrounded by the remains of the meat course which he was bringing from the dining room. As he has put his foot up to push the door from one side, Valour took a flying leap from the other and sent Faithfull and his tray flying.

We girls always took 'my' Valour with us when going for a walk. On one of my half days I thought I would give him a really good airing. It was a lovely day. We went on the bus to Beverley, about three miles away, and I intended walking back.

We just got through Beverley Bar on our return when he set off like a jet with me hanging on to the lead. He was yelping, everyone was looking at us, I didn't know what to do. I just hoped he would soon stop. He then started having diarrhoea.

By this time I was feeling very embarrassed. A lady working

in her front garden came to my rescue with a bowl of water for him, but he didn't want it. She said he had hysteria and that I must get him home quickly, a bit difficult when 'home' was three miles away. So I went back to Beverley to a taxi owner I knew and he took us back to Etton Hall.

I had to battle with Valour all the way. He was jumping all over the back of that taxi still yelping loudly. I realised afterwards I had been in some danger of being bitten but my only thought was to get him home and some attention for him.

When we arrived at the Hall, I thought it would be rather difficult to get him out of the taxi in the state he was in. So I asked the driver to ring the front door bell as the Major was away. My intention was to get Faithfull to hold the lead while I got out. To my horror, Faithfull released him, and Valour did a couple of mad circuits round the lawn, then collapsed and died. It took me a long time to get over that experience and the dog's death.

There were masses of flowers and plants in my stately homes all year round. The gardeners provided everything from a buttonhole to a wreath for a funeral. I remember Etton Hall for red carnations. Major Hillas always wore one. There was a special greenhouse at the Hall just for growing them. Every morning a fresh carnation was brought in by the head gardener, and put in a small vase on the front hall table for the Major to pick up as he went out. If he returned for lunch or tea and was going out again, there would be a fresh one brought in. The Major's partner of the Hunt, Captain Bethell, favoured a white carnation.

Flowers filled the huge entrance hall of Etton Hall. At Christmas there were white chrysanthemums about 5ft tall, with curled heads as big as tea plates. Even now white chrysanthemums make me think of Christmas. Another thing the gardeners did at Christmas was to make a lengthy garland of evergreens, which was looped all the way up the banisters of the front stairs and the gallery around the front landing, also twined around the three stone pillars in the hall. At Christmas of 1939, the hall looked even lovelier with a huge tree reaching up the well of the stairs, the tip of it level with the top rail of the gallery. That particular year the Major gave a party for his grandchildren, which no doubt proved to be the one and only. At that time we were in the period of the phoney war; even rationing hadn't started then.

At Christmas, a custom started by Mrs Hillas and continued by the Major was to give all the widows of the village 1lb tea and 5s each. This may sound trivial in these days but when it is remembered that a widow's pension was about 10s per week, it was an acceptable gift. The children from the village school used to stand in a half circle around the front hall fire singing carols. They were each given a bag of sweets, an apple, orange and a sixpence. In those days this was a great treat, as the average child was more accustomed to the humble halfpenny, which was always spent with great care.

Up the staircase were some fascinating prints of the 'First Steeple Chase on Record'. If I remember rightly, it was at Ipswich run by moonlight, and the riders wore what looked like nightshirts and pointed sleeping caps! Around the gallery was a set of twelve cries of London, of which I was particularly fond.

Across from the butler's pantry was the glass room where all the glassware was kept. Table glass of all kinds included a set of Hartlepool 'Ship' glass for Claret, Hock, Port, Champagne, Brandy, Sherry and liqueurs. Even at that time they were of considerable value and only used on very special occasions. Each glass was engraved with a ship of the 'Windjammer' class. I was interested to see one on TV's 'Going for a Song'.

There were also some very beautiful Lalique finger bowls and flower vases. The Major also had the nicest fish plates I have ever seen. Each plate had a different fish, hand-painted in the centre; around the edge of the plate were shells cut in the china deep enough to hold sauce.

Major Hillas had two 'shoots', the further one being on Gardham Moor for grouse. As this was some considerable distance away, the lunch went up with the guns. The hot meal and plates were packed in hay boxes to keep them hot. Soup and vegetables were taken in gallon-sized Thermos flasks. The vegetables were put into aluminium containers shaped to fit inside the Thermos.

Faithfull went with them on these occasions and was away all day. When the shoot was at Goodmanham, only a few miles away, the chauffeur who loaded for the Major used to come back in the car to take Faithfull (what a ridiculously apt name for a butler!) and the lunch.

Most of the guns, that is the gentlemen of the shooting party, travelled in the shooting brake, which had a long seat down each side and in the floor two sockets where a table was set up for the meal.

The beaters went on a truck and the game was brought back on that. If the Major saw one of the villagers as they returned, he would call to him, 'Want a rabbit?' and toss one to him. At intervals during the season we were given the choice of a hare or a couple of rabbits to take home.

Anyone living too far away from home had them sent through the post which, in those days, was a postal service to be proud of. I doubt if anyone would dare send game through the post now. It would walk to its destination before it was delivered! The game was packed into a bass bag of straw, stitched along the top with a label attached addressed to the recipient. All this was done by Smith, the chauffeur, and taken to the post by him. The Major paid the postage.

At the end of the day, the gentlemen retired to the study for a drink and to discuss the 'bag'. Meanwhile, the loaders ate a hot meal in the servants' hall. There was always a substantial lunch sent out to the loaders as well as the guns.

A treasure of Etton Hall I much admired consisted of a pair of vases on the drawing room mantelpiece. They were about 2ft high, encrusted with china flowers, and a gorgeous coloured bird formed the handle of the lid.

Another precious piece was in the best guest room, standing on a table between the twin beds: a china Gainsborough lady table lamp, with the large picture hat and lovely gown of the period, which had lace flounces and rose buds all made of china. Her pink parasol was the lamp shade. In most houses when guest rooms were not in use, all the ornaments, racks of note paper, ink stands and books were put away in the wardrobes or drawers and the furniture dust-sheeted.

But there is no doubt that the greatest treasure of Etton Hall was the incredibly named Faithfull. Some years before Major and Mrs Hillas went their separate ways, Faithfull's son was born. Mrs Hillas asked what name he had chosen. When he replied, 'Brian, madam,' she replied, 'Just Brian?' 'Yes, madam.' 'Oh! You must give him a second name or his initials will be B.F.—b-fool!' So Neil was added as a second name.

# 12
# Silly Old Devil

'Silly old devil' was Faithfull's pet name for Major Hillas. It was affectionately meant, but on the morning that the Major set the dining room curtains on fire he may have used the name somewhat impatiently!

As usual the Major had been for his pre-breakfast ride, taking all the dogs with him, and he had got back about 9.30am. I was turning out the front hall with my under-housemaid when he came in. He started breakfast, but in a few minutes rushed out, calling for Faithfull.

There were flames up to the dining room ceiling. The hot plate and the Cona coffee maker with their spirit burners stood on the serving table in the big square bay window. He upset them, and the meths ran along the cloth on to the floor, spreading the flames up the curtain. Major Hillas ripped down the curtain and stamped on it, and just one curtain and the tablecloth got burned.

Faithfull came out of the dining room laughing his head off. 'Silly old devil set fire to the curtain,' he said.

The Major always wore white cotton socks under his coloured ones. One morning when we were making his bed and the old butler was putting the master's evening clothes away he said: 'Silly old devil said last evening I had put him only one white sock out. Silly old devil had two white socks on one foot!'

The Major was very particular about his shirts. He wore pure silk cream ones in the daytime. These and his evening shirts were sent each week by post in special boxes to a laundry in London. Not only were they immaculately laundered, but kept impeccably repaired.

When working at his office as a timber importer, the Major used to lunch at the Station Hotel in Hull. During Easter week of 1939, he met the comedian Tom Walls, who was staying there while playing the lead in *It's a Boy* at the Alexander Theatre. As both gentlemen were owners of racehorses, they became acquainted. There being no performance on Good Friday, Tom Walls and his leading lady were invited to dinner; also in the party were Captain Bethell and Mr and Mrs Keith Hillas.

The main course of the dinner was pheasant. We housemaids and Tom Walls's chauffeur were sitting in the servants' hall. Suddenly down the passage from the kitchen came the cook in great agitation, shouting, 'My oven's on fire. My oven's on fire!'

The chauffeur dashed out into the yard and scooped up a shovel full of gravel, rushed into the kitchen, opened the oven door and flung the lot in. 'Oh! My pheasants, my pheasants,' she cried. 'So and so your pheasants. You wanted the fire out, didn't you?'

There was gravel and soil in the roasting tin with the pheasants, but they still went in for dinner in that state. I hope Mr Walls was not gravelly-voiced at his next performance!

Etton Hall was on a slight rise at one end of the village, so that we looked down on it. Often during autumn and winter evenings I used to look down at the cottages as dusk was falling and see the lights appearing in the windows, and smoke rising from the chimneys. It looked such a picture of peace and contentment. I could visualise the families sitting down to tea, beside a cosy fire and think how lovely it must be to have one's own little place and someone who really cares.

Sometimes now when my husband and I are out strolling with our dog down our little lane and I see the lights and smoke of our neighbours' cottages, I think of that scene from my room at Etton Hall.

A memory picture of my beloved countryside I can readily recapture is that of the Yorkshire Wolds in 1939 when the winter was very severe. It was a beautiful sight with snow 'meringues' along the dyke sides and miniature igloos whipped up by the wind. Many roads were blocked and in spite of large gangs of men out digging the Market Weighton road, it never was cleared until the thaw came in March. Etton village pond was frozen to a depth of 3ft. The village folk used to cycle and walk across it taking a short cut to the Cherry Burton road.

The thaw, when it came, was a rapid one with which the drains could not cope, so the village became flooded. We, being on a slight rise, were thankfully high and dry. The ice on the pond broke up and floated like miniature icebergs down the village street. As the flood water receded, these were left blocking the main road through the village, causing traffic diversions. Tractors from the farms near by towed the ice on to the grass verges.

While at Etton I started taking lessons in voice production. I have always enjoyed singing and consider the human voice one of the lovelist musical instruments. I wished to improve my voice for my own pleasure. Hilda had whetted my appetite for something a little more worthwhile than musical potato peeling! Alas, the war intervened. The lady who taught me, uncertain of her own future, cancelled all lessons.

I was shortly to 'sing a different tune' in a different kind of uniform.

In the early days of the phoney war we had three army officers billeted with us, a colonel, an adjutant and a young captain. With Major Hillas frequently away, they had full use of the house, except for his bedroom, bathroom and study.

The colonel had his hunter stabled in one of the loose boxes. A private groomed and exercised it each day. His batman, who was billeted with him at the hunt kennels in the village, came morning and evening to valet the colonel. This, indeed, was soldiering in luxury!

A housemaid does not have a sitting down job. When I think of a domestic seated, it's Alice, the head housemaid of Rise, who comes to mind, sitting grandly in her Windsor armchair in the housemaids' pantry, with her feet comfortably placed on her footstool which one of us had to put in position.

It was my job to have the kettle boiling by 10am for the mid-morning tea break, and I laid the table with cups and saucers, and cake and scones. I was not considered capable of brewing the tea, that was Alice's business.

Emma the housemaid sat on her stool to drink her tea, I made do with the bottom step of the stairs up to our bedroom.

Thinking of people seated reminds me of loos I have heard of and ones that I have known. Some of the loos in country houses had alarming names like 'Deluge' and 'Niagara', and a friend in domestic service remembers one with the name of a famous loo manufacturer on the cistern: T. Crapper, Chelsea, London.

I have known loos disguised as boxes and chairs, and I was told of one pedestal moulded in the form of a lion. You sat on the lion's head to spend a penny, and hoped he would not bite! Another pedestal was shaped like a dolphin with his tail up. Many pedestals had floral decorations, often in a deep—almost indigo—blue, and white. Or the flowers to be sat upon were in a raised pattern. I have heard of daffodils 'in relief' around a pedestal! Moulded oak leaves and acorns sometimes adorn a pedestal in a patriotic design!

All the toilets at the Keppels' at Windsor, and some at Rise, had a wooden casing round them. In the front of the house they were of polished wood and in the back scrubbed white wood was usual. When closed they looked like a blanket chest, and were worked by a brass handle, kept polished, and pulled upwards like a plunger. The baths in the front bathrooms at the Keppels' were on a dias, and they had a polished wooden case round them.

It was Skipton Castle which had the most memorable of the

old sanitary arrangements I came across. Kitchen refuse and ashes went into the moat, which also used to receive offerings from an old second floor toilet. That loo, in a part of the castle not used for centuries, was known as the 'long drop'.

I took the temporary post at the castle while awaiting call up. It was then the home of Captain Fordyce, the land agent, and his family. The days of the mansion with a host of servants were over. Shortage of staff was already being felt at Skipton. I was sharing a roof with British Museum treasures stored there for the duration.

The great castle is one of the most complete and best preserved in the country. It has a 50ft long banqueting hall, and a big kitchen with hearths for baking and roasting. The balustrade over the gatehouse is surmounted by the family motto in letters of stone: Desormais (henceforth).

By the time I arrived there Skipton Castle was henceforth to be understaffed. The days of its being run as a great residence might just as well have been back in the fourteenth century when the Clifford family took possession.

How many of my stately homes are now visited by the public, paying an admission fee to admire the pictures and other works of art within, and the flowers and gardens without?

Skipton Castle survives as a magnet for the sightseer. Its grotto room of stone and pearly shells and the dungeon are considerable attractions. In my time at the castle an odd job man showed visitors round. Adults were charged 6d and children 4d.

The Skipton local authority decided not to buy the castle in the 1950s when the estate was sold by Lord Hothfield. 'We do not buy expense', was given as their reason. A group of local residents got together to run the castle, and today the ancient bastion, once my home, is visited by 90,000 people each year.

From a fortress which protected an ancient family to one of the Forces defending the country. I became a WAAF.

I wanted to learn to drive and applied for transport duties. But at a half inch more than 5ft I was too small.

'What was your work as a civilian?' I was asked.

When I told them I was in domestic service they made me a batwoman.

# 13
# Changed Times

It was at Middlethorpe Hall that I returned to private service after the war. In spite of its great age, I do not think Skipton Castle was haunted, but Middlethorpe Hall, an eighteenth-century house near York, was reputed to have a ghost. There was plenty of room for one! A considerable staff ran the house before the war, now reduced to four and a nanny. Colonel Stobart and family lived there.

Things were greatly changed. The cost of running a large house together with rationing, especially of heating fuel, made it necessary to close a considerable section of the house, so only a few rooms were occupied. Women, who had learned new skills and had a wider range of trades open to them, were more than ever reluctant to do domestic work.

At Middlethorpe Hall there was a young Irish cook, a parlour-maid who had been with the family for twenty years, known affectionately as 'Birdie', her sister who did the personal laundry for the lady and gentleman of the house and helped her sister in the dining room when we had guests. I was housemaid and there was an elderly woman living in the bothy in the courtyard who was nursery-maid.

Many of the front rooms were no longer in use. A small sitting room was used for meals, the dining room being used only on the few occasions when there were visitors. The kitchen, scullery, servants' hall and larders were all shut up, the butler's pantry was made into a kitchen and a small room leading off it fitted with cupboards to serve as a larder. We took our meals in the kitchen and sat there when off duty.

When I went there in 1945 the house had been sold and a small estate had been purchased in Durham, to which we moved. Headlam Hall was a lovely Elizabethan house with lots of gables and mullioned windows. There was also a home farm and eight cottages. I do not know the acreage of land. I was told by Birdie, who was usually well informed, that the whole had been purchased for £20,000, which looks silly by today's prices.

The move came as a great relief to me. Middlethorpe's reputation for being haunted and the accounts of strange happenings began to unnerve me. I never saw or heard anything unusual, but I was sensitive to atmosphere and the stories were affecting my health. Had we not moved I could not have stayed with this family.

I shall never forget that removal operation. Transferring the contents of a house the size of Middlethorpe was an immense undertaking. In addition the contents of the two cottages occupied by Birdie, her sister and aged aunt, and the head gardener and his wife, had to go to Durham. What was in the outbuildings and the garden and garage equipment were part of the transfer! Every day for two weeks two giant pantechnicons travelled up to Headlam. The foreman of the removers was a gigantic chap by the name of Theodore. He could upend a full chest of drawers, put an arm round two legs and carry it out. He moved a dining table in the same way. Whenever his mates had difficulty in getting a piece of furniture through a door a cry would go up for Theodore's advice, which was always the same, 'Tha's gotta 'umour it!' 'Umour it he did, with apparent ease. This became a catchphrase with us for any difficult situation.

We did not take with us the two stone birds which sat on the roof at Middlethorpe. Most people thought they were eagles.

They were, in fact, bustards, and were once embellishments for a big house in a neighbouring hamlet, now vanished. I visited the site of the hamlet. It was called Bustardthorpe!

There was an extraordinary happening when Sir Richard and Lady Graham stayed at Headlam Hall one weekend for a hunt ball held a few miles way. The ball was on a Saturday night, and they returned home on the following Monday. When packing for Lady Graham I could find only one of her diamond earrings. When I mentioned this to her she explained that she had lost the other one at the ball, and that she was worried since she had already made an insurance claim for a lost diamond ring. She felt that she could not put in another claim so soon.

That evening the telephone rang at the hall, and I answered it. Lady Graham was telephoning to say that her earring had been found. There had been a lot of rain in the week preceding the ball, and the Grahams' car was parked in a very muddy spot. When they arrived home the chauffeur washed the car, and a lump of mud fell off one of the wheels. Embedded in it was the missing earring! It had travelled stuck to the wheel all the way from Headlam near Darlington to Norton Conyers near Ripon.

The household had been increased by one when we moved to Headlam. The young cook at Middlethorpe got married, so did not accompany us. The wife of one of the farm workers and an elderly friend of hers now came in daily as cook and kitchenmaid. This was typical of the improvisation that went on during the time that the great houses were becoming too big to live in, and staffs had dwindled.

Headlam was isolated, bus and train services almost nonexistent. I had seen very little of my sister Hilda during the war. She was working in Leicestershire, so I took a post in that county to be near her. It was there that I met my husband.

When I went to Leicestershire to join the household of Mr and Mrs Philip Johnson of Tur Langton, my sister was cook at Stone House, Blaston, near Market Harborough, a post she was to hold for sixteen years.

My employer was a gentleman farmer. Colonel Phillip

Henry Lloyd, joint master of the Fernie Hunt and chairman of Leicestershire County Council was my sister's employer.

His family founded Lloyd's bank and owned collieries and steel mills. He used to tell a fascinating story connected with the ill-fated mills at Corby, closed as a nationalised enterprise.

At the time of the Great Exhibition of 1851 his grandfather heard a lecture on iron ore deposits. Thirty years later he was travelling from Nottingham to London when the train broke down in a cutting. He looked out of the window and saw something which reminded him of that lecture. He jumped down and nicked a sample of rock which analysts later found was 80 per cent iron ore. The Corby steel works were founded on that petty pilfery!

Although Colonel Lloyd was connected with the family coal mines and saw to the mechanisation of some Yorkshire ones, he was a true countryman and a farmer. I am glad that he hated the pulling out of hedges as 'desecration' of the countryside. He called it 'crazy', as I do.

Travelling to Leicestershire to my new post, and looking forward to seeing Hilda, I remembered the happy times my sister and I had spent in service together, how the worst that had happened was nothing more than soup mistakenly thrown away. I remembered how being a tweeny meant being able to do compensatory duties with Hilda which made up for having to help stern old Alice.

Mrs Beeton said a cook must possess the qualities of cleanliness, neatness, order, regularity and celerity of action. The maids assisting her must be ready, willing, tidy and 'active in their movements'.

I am sure that both Hilda and I measured up to these requirements. The difficulty in post-war houses was the lack of assistance!

Reading Beeton some time ago, I was amused to see what she had to say about the 'larger establishments of the middle ages'. Cooks with the authority of feudal chiefs gave their orders from a high chair commanding a view of all that was going on. Each held a long wooden spoon with which to taste the food being prepared, and it was something used as a rod to punish the idle. Hilda would have hated to hold such office. But that exercise of authority would have just suited Alice!

In spite of that lady I remember Rise with affection. Big house, big staff, splendid food and lodging, beautiful park. Truly the time of a tweeny's life!

# 14
# Having a Ball

Never again would there be such entertaining as in the pre-war years. Never again such hosts—or guests!

The affluence of some guests was breathtaking. It used to take three Rolls Royces to bring two talked-about sisters to one country house I knew. They never visited for more than two nights, but what a retinue! One of the sisters was rather advanced for those days. She was able to drive and insisted on doing so.

The pair came in that year's Rolls, their head chauffeur followed in the previous year's model (in case of a puncture or other mishap). The second chauffeur, two lady's maids with their own luggage and the ladies' jewels in the third Rolls, and to complete the convoy, the third chauffeur with luggage in a Humber shooting brake!

The big houses were full of music and colour at party time. The hunt balls kept a large staff and extra help on the go. A top London band was hired for the night, and it certainly was a night to remember! First, there was a big dinner party for the family and the guests staying in the house.

A cold buffet supper was served about 2am and was there all the time for anyone who wanted it. A champagne bar was open all the time, and food and drink for all the workers, chauffeurs and anyone else who was helping. Breakfast was served from 4am to 5am, eggs, bacon, sausages, kidney.

A typical dinner was soup, fish, meat, sweet, savoury. When asparagus or globe artichokes were in season they were served as a separate course. If guests were staying there was sometimes an additional course, and in the case of a big dinner party maybe two or three courses extra. The savoury was followed by dessert, consisting of fresh fruit in season. Salted nuts and liqueur chocolates were also available.

During the meal, a different wine was served with each course: sherry with soup, dry white wine with fish, claret or Burgundy with the meat, depending on what it was, then a sweet wine offered with the sweet. If champagne was being drunk, sherry was served with the soup, then champagne for the rest of the meal.

After the dessert the ladies retired to the drawing room for coffee. Port and cigars were handed round to the gentlemen, then the butler and footman left the room, the gentlemen probably talking for an hour or more.

The foregoing suggests a tremendous amount of food, but the portions were only small, and a long time would be taken over the meal. It was served at 8pm and the eating was over by, perhaps, 9.30pm (if dinner was on time). It could be 11 or 11.30pm before the dining room was cleared.

When there was a big shooting party, there were a number of visiting servants. A valet was called by his gentleman's name. Seating at table was according to his master's rank. The valet of a Lord was superior to one whose master was a 'Sir', and a 'Sir's' valet came before one of a mister or one whose gentleman was a military man.

If the local hunt met at the house all the mounted followers were offered a drink—port, sherry, cherry brandy, sloe gin, with whisky for the huntsmen and whips, and others who asked for it. I longed to try the sloe gin, which was made in the house. Alas, it was locked in the butler's pantry.

In houses with upwards of twenty in staff, a servants' ball was held around Christmas time. The ball started with the gentleman of the house having the first dance with the cook and his lady danced with the butler. My sister dropped an awful brick at a house where she was head kitchen-maid. The eldest son of the family asked her for the first dance. Not knowing who he was, she said she was engaged for that turn around the floor! The mistake is readily explained. Except for the butler's pantry staff and the lady's maid, the rest of the servants very rarely saw the family, the kitchen staff least of all.

Master and mistress stayed for about half an hour and after a toast to them they left. The ball then got going, but was fairly respectable and sober until the butler, cook and their guests had gone. After that, it was really enjoyable! As the ball did not usually start until about 10pm we were out of bed for most of the night. It was work again in the morning, and a case of wash and change and into uniform for a day's duty without sleep, but not without sustenance. There would no doubt be some tasty leftovers.

What mouthwatering odours I can recall from assisting Hilda in the kitchen! I have written about nostalgic smells, and gathering material for the following pages brought back many appetising aromas of cooking. Some of this culinary fragrance is associated with particular seasons . . .

# Dinner Menus

## Spring

*Clear soup with vegetables*
*Fish patties*
*Roast pheasant*
*Game chips    Brussels sprouts*
*Claret jelly with cream*
*Cream cheese savoury*

*Bonne femme (leek) soup*
*Fried sole with orange sauce*
*Ragout of lamb*
*Green peas    Duchesse potatoes*
*Compote of pears*
*Devilled chicken livers*

*Plovers' eggs*
*Roast fillet of veal*
*Salad*
*Pêches à la Melba*
*Cheese aigrettes*

## Summer

*Hollandaise soup*
*Sole in aspic*
*Roast lamb*
*Green peas    New potatoes*
*Gooseberry fool    Cats' tongues*
*Anchovy straws*

*Asparagus soup*
*Chicken and ham cutlets*
*Blanquette of veal*
*Potatoes with cream and cheese*
*Raspberry and red currant tart*
*Cheese canapés*

*Clear soup*
*Boiled turbot    Shrimp sauce*
*Beef olives*
*Vegetable marrow with cream sauce*
*Coffee éclairs*
*Cheese straws*

## Autumn

*Kidney soup*
*Stewed scallops*
*Chicken à la hongroise*
*Pineapple fritters*
*Ham croûtes*

*Oysters*
*Tomato soup*
*Grilled cutlets    Potato ribbons*
*Cranberry mould*
*Cods roe à la Victoria*

*Cream of corn soup*
*Fish soufflé*
*Venison en casserole*
*Brussels sprouts    Duchesse potatoes*
*Coffee meringue pudding*
*Devils on horseback*

## Winter

*Chicken soup*
*Fish quenelles*
*Fillets of beef*
*Japanese artichokes*
*Stewed Normandy pippins*
*Whipped cream*
*Sardines à la piedmontaise*

*Rice and tomato soup*
*Fillets of plaice with green peas*
*Salmi of game*
*Potato fritters*
*Pear and chestnut tart*
*Cheese ramequins*

*Mutton broth*
*Stuffed fillets of haddock*
*Curried chicken    Boiled rice*
*Cold apricot soufflé*
*Savoury brain croûtes*

There seems to have been a rule not to have a white meat following a white fish, or a light-coloured sweet following a white meat.

# Luncheon Menus

## Spring

*Cauliflower soufflé*
*Cold beef with mixed salad*
*Apple fool*
*Sponge fingers*

*Savoury omelet*
*Fricassee of rabbit*
*Banana fritters*

*Eggs in aspic*
*Oxtail stew*
*Rhubarb fool in glasses*

## Summer

*Dressed crab*
*Stewed lamb*
*Gooseberry tart*

*Lobster mayonnaise*
*Grilled fillets of beef*
*Strawberry shortcake*

*Cheese omelet*
*Chaudfroid of chicken*
*Banana pudding*

## Autumn

*Halibut with cream sauce*
*Meat and macaroni timbale*
*Claret jelly*

*Tomatoes with curried rice*
*Galantine of curried chicken*
*Chocolate pudding*

*Grilled mackerel*
*Beef olives*
*Baked tomatoes*
*Custard tartlets*
*Compote of pears*

## Winter

*Stuffed fillets of fish*
*Russian steaks*
*Apple charlotte*

*Savoury pancakes*
*Stewed venison*
*Apple tart*

*Golden eggs*
*Turkey legs devilled*
*French pancakes*

At luncheon there was always a cold ham and a tongue on the sideboard.

# Breakfast Menus

For breakfast tea, coffee and porridge were usual. Also there was always a cold ham and a tongue, and either boiled eggs or eggs to boil with a small spirit stove on the sideboard.

*Bacon and eggs*
*Fish cakes*
*Curried mushrooms*

*Fresh herrings fried*
*Bath chap*
*Bacon and eggs*

*Bloaters*
*Savoury omelet*
*Potted game*

*Chicken and ham kedgeree*
*Kidney omelet*
*Potted cods roe*

*Smoked haddock kedgeree*
*Bacon and mushrooms*
*Scrambled eggs*

*Grilled kidneys, bacon*
*Raised veal and ham pie*
*Potted salmon*

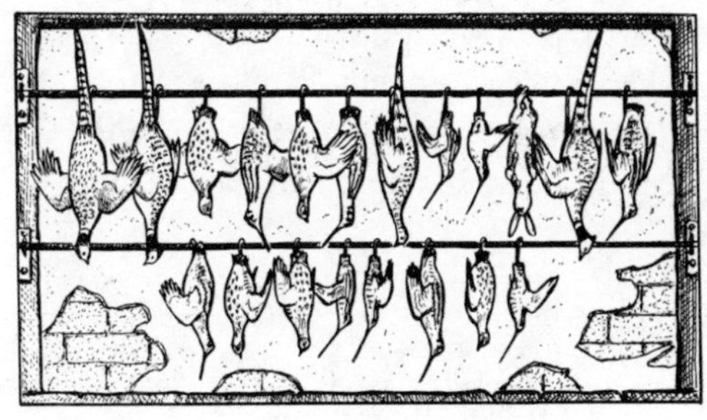

# 15
# In Her Own Hand

My brother-in-law has Hilda's cookery books, which I have been thoroughly interested to read and reread, particularly the notebook in her handwriting containing her own ideas, as well as her modifications—just as original—to traditional recipes.

These pages in the handwriting I know so well bring back all kinds of memories of delicious food, from rich feasts of many courses to cocktail snacks. Not all of it was tasted by the servants, although they had their treats, including venison and some game birds. Much of it we just saw, or savoured by the nose!

Many of the ingredients were subtle (unnecessary, the modern, budget-watching housewife will say), but Hilda was a magician who could change the character of a dish simply by substituting one ingredient (perhaps through necessity) and I have known occasions when she was congratulated for such a switch. Some of the ingredients are a little mysterious. What, for instance, is prunella? I assume it is the herb self-heal (*Prunella vulgaris*), which has antiseptic and astringent properties.

Cooking in Hilda's day needed dedication and stamina. It was a time before culinary materials and embellishments were available in tins and packets, and everything had to be 'made'.

Please note too that some of the temperatures quoted refer to cooking with an Esse stove (similar to an Aga).

I remember Hilda's aspic jelly, and her meat glaze for coating cooked hams and tongue. I can still see the glaze in a big stone jar. This is how she made it, according to her handwritten cook book:

**Meat Glaze**

Good quality brown stock, free from grease, can be used, especially bone stock, as it is more glutinous. Allow to boil fast, without the pan lid, to reduce to half quantity, skimming as often as needed. Strain and put into a smaller pan, and boil until stock becomes as thick as treacle and a good brown colour. It is then ready for use. Can be stored in a stone jar. With a little melted lard poured over the top it will keep several weeks.

*Before the days of self-raising flour, Hilda even had her own recipe for what she calls:*

**Superior Baking Flour**

4oz bicarbonate of soda
3oz tartaric acid
1oz cream of tartar

Sieve well together and keep in an airtight tin.

*For cakes and sweets she grated Chocolate Menier, and if this was not available she resorted to chocolate powder. One of her unbreakable rules was puff pastry for meat pies, mince pies and sausage rolls. She used leaf gelatin a great deal.*

**Aspic Jelly**

1½pt good stock, free from grease
1 gill (¼pt) sherry
1 gill vinegar
1-1½oz leaf gelatin
rind and juice of one lemon
pieces of carrot, turnip and celery
a bouquet garni
few peppercorns and cloves

whites and shells of 2 eggs
salt

Into a pan put the stock and gelatin broken in small pieces. Add vegetables and herbs, sherry, whites of eggs and crushed shells. Add the vinegar, salt, lemon rind peeled very thin and the strained juice. Stir over heat until frothy and almost boil, then leave at the side of stove for 10 min with the lid on, then strain.

**Béchamel Sauce**

Hilda suggests Béchamel sauce for various dishes. This French sauce can be made with 2oz butter, 2oz flour, 1pt milk, salt and pepper—the pepper is important.

Cook the flour and butter, mixed well, over moderate heat until golden. Remove from heat, add the cold milk, stir well and return to heat. Keep on stirring until the sauce thickens. Season generously.

**Garnishes for Grills**

Embellishments Hilda used included *parsley butter,* made by adding finely chopped parsley to butter, mixing well with a knife. It can be served with fried sole. (After cooking make a slit to receive it.) The parsley butter should be shaped into a roll with butter pats. It goes well with steak.

Colonel Lloyd used to like fried bananas with fillet steak. Hilda sliced the bananas, and fried them without batter.

**Spiced Peaches**
(To serve with cold ham, pork, chicken or turkey)

15oz tin peaches
3 tabsp vinegar
6-8 cloves
demerara sugar to taste
stick of cinnamon

Make a sauce with the peach juice, vinegar, demerara sugar, cinnamon. Boil till thick and pour over peaches.

*Hilda needed a fair knowledge of butchery. She had pig, sheep and lamb carcases brought to her from the home farms, as well as beef and venison, and she had to know how to deal with them.*

*As to venison, the flesh of the fallow deer is considered the best, usually from animals four to five years old. It should always be well hung, and in cold dry weather can hang for two weeks or longer according to taste. It should be wiped and sprinkled with black pepper, and tested periodically for freshness by running a skewer into the flesh near the bone. If it is free from smell and stickiness, it is in good condition.*

*The cook book contains directions for what Hilda calls:*

**Pickle for a Pig (or Full-sized Ham)**

2lb salt
3oz bay leaves
1oz prunella
1oz saltpetre
1lb dark treacle
½lb coarse sugar

At least four times this for a whole pig.

Mix sugar, treacle, prunella, saltpetre and bay leaves together and stand for twenty-four hours. Rub pig with the common salt for three days. Drain salt away. Rub well with pickle. Turn daily. Pickling times: streaky, four days; back, ten days; ham, three to four weeks. Then hang to dry.

*Many of the dishes in the book contain cream, and others require so many ingredients that most housewives would not use them even occasionally.*

*An example is the spaghetti bolognese recipe supplied by whoever was the Grosvenor Hotel chef at the time. It was given to Hilda by a guest of the Lloyds at Blaston, who was delighted with one of Hilda's variations on a classic theme.*

**Spaghetti Bolognese**

4oz liver or kidney
3-4oz spaghetti per person
1lb lean gammon
2 tabsp olive oil
4 finely chopped onions
small clove garlic, finely chopped
2-4oz sliced mushrooms
5½oz tin tomato purée
pinch of fresh dried tarragon
1pt meat or bone stock
2 tabsp red wine or sherry

Mince meat, heat oil, add onion and garlic. Cook gently 4-5 min, till slightly coloured. Add mushrooms, then meat. Cook quickly, stirring once or twice until meat is set and has changed colour. Stir in tomato purée and tarragon, add wine and stock. Simmer gently 1-1¼ hours. Cook spaghetti in fast boiling water for 20 min. Strain, toss in clean pan with a little oil. Serve on hot dish with sauce poured over.

*Housewives for whom stock, tomato purée and onions will do, added to the meat, will find the above grossly extravagant, as well as some of the dishes requiring cream.*

**Cream of Beef**

Raw beef pounded in a pestle and mortar after mincing
1 egg
pepper and salt
finely chopped onion
Cream

Add the egg to the pounded beef, and pass through a wire sieve. Season with pepper and salt, add chopped onion. Mix cream with it to the consistency of whipped cream, put into a mould and steam for one hour.

For the sauce, thicken a little good stock, add some tomato sauce, Worcester sauce and Harvey's sauce. Pour over.

Creamed rabbit can be prepared in the same way, but with Béchamel sauce.

**Spanish Blancmange**

6oz sugar
2oz lemon sugar
2pt cream
½pt water
juice of one lemon
1oz isinglass
1 teacup (¼pt) warm water

Mix sugar and lemon sugar with 1pt of the cream. Add the water and juice of lemon, and stir until the sugar has dissolved, then stir in the other pint of cream. Dissolve the isinglass in the teacup of warm water, mix with the rest of the ingredients and stir over top of stove until warm, then pour into mould.

*Now how's the following for extravagance? You may remember that I once threw Hilda's last drop of it down the sink!*

**Clear Soup (Consommé Julienne)**

3lb shin beef
1lb knuckle veal
3 quarts water
1 carrot
1 turnip
2 onions
2 leeks
few sticks of celery
a bunch of herbs
few peppercorns
few cloves
salt and pepper

Keeping the proportion of water 1 quart to each lb meat, cut up the meat; break up any bones as far as possible to extract all goodness. Leave to soak in the water for ½ hour, then put on the stove. Bring slowly to the boil, then adjust heat to simmer. After ½ hour, skimming can begin to remove scum. After an hour, if clear of scum, add other ingredients, with the herbs tied in a muslin bag.

This would simmer at the side of the stove for the best part of a week, *without the lid* or it would become cloudy. Hilda used to clear her soup with crushed egg shells. Before serving, sherry would be added to the tureen together with the garnish, this usually being cooked vegetables cut in wafer-thin shapes and dropped into the tureen.

*Time-consuming as well as expensive, but here's a cocktail party quickie, or a starter:*

**Eggs Baked in Tomatoes**

large tomatoes
1 egg per tomato
1 small minced onion
½ finely chopped sweet green pepper
chopped parsley

Cut the top off the tomatoes. Scoop out to hold egg. In the cavity place the onion, pepper and parsley. Break an egg into each tomato, sit them close together on a baking sheet and bake until white of egg is set. Serve with brown sauce.

*More starters, or cocktail snacks:*

**Sardine Spread**

Skin and bone large sardines. Mash them and add an equal amount of margarine or butter, working in a little oil from the can. Add pepper and a dash of Worcester sauce.

**Shellfish Snacks**

Dice shellfish, dress with tomato sauce, cream and lemon juice. To fill sandwiches, finely shredded lettuce may be added. For cocktails, spread on thin toast cut in fingers and rounds or on cracker biscuits.

**Drumsticks—1**

Bone each drum stick and stuff with sausage meat mixed with grated orange. Put drumsticks into oven dish, and cover with red wine sauce. Bake 30-40 min at 350°F.

**Sauce**

1/4pt water
1/2pt red wine
juice of one orange

**Drumsticks—2**

boned fresh drumsticks
1 small onion
equal quantities of chicken stuffing and sausage meat
orange juice and grated rind

Chop and fry onion in butter till soft. Add flour to thicken. When cooked add orange juice and rind, water and wine. Simmer 20-30 min. Put drumsticks in dish with sauce. Cover with lid or foil. Bake 30-40 min at 350°F. Test with skewer.

**Haddock Bouchées**

6 cheese pastry cases, cooked
3oz cooked fresh haddock
2 teasp chutney
2 tabsp white sauce

Mix all ingredients and fill pastry cases with the mixture. Garnish with sliced gherkins. Serve hot or cold.

**Herring or Pilchard Bouchées**

6 cheese pastry cases and lids
2 tinned herrings or pilchards
1 tabsp tomato purée
4 chopped gherkins
salt, pepper, cayenne

Fill cases as before, but cover with pastry lids and glaze with egg. Leave for ½ hour. Cook in hot oven, 420°F.

**Kipper Tartlets**

cheese pastry cases, cooked
kipper fillets
olive oil and vinegar
chopped shallots

Mix oil, vinegar and shallots. Add kipper fillets to marinate overnight. The following day, remove kipper fillets. Chop finely and fill pastry cases. Makes a good savoury, as well as being useful for cocktails.

**Fondue Parmesan**

3½oz butter
2oz flour
5½oz grated parmesan cheese
boiling water
2 egg yolks

Melt the butter, add flour. Mix well. Add boiling water gradually and egg yolks, beating to éclair mixture consistency, so that the fondue leaves the pan in a ball. All this while heating. Take off heat, add cheese and leave to cool in a flat dish. When cool, cut into seven or eight pieces. Coat in breadcrumbs and fry.

*Seafood is prominent, indeed dominant, in Hilda's book of culinary secrets. The following recipe is so luxurious that it might as well remain a secret from the practical point of view, but it makes pleasant reading as culinary fantasy:*

**Fillets of Sole in Lobster Cream**

Allow 1 fillet of sole per person
1 or 2 lobsters according to number of guests
(First, catch one lobster!)
1 egg
cream

Take lobster out of shell and mince. Trim sole fillets, add them to lobster and mince both together two or three times. Add a little cream and stiffly beaten egg white (may need a little yolk as well). Line mould with sole fillets and fill with lobster cream. Steam very slowly until cooked. Serve with sauce.

*Perhaps mock crab is more suitable for today's comparative austerity:*

**Cottage Crab**

1lb hake
2oz shrimps
2 eggs
1oz butter
salt and pepper
mustard

Steam hake, flake, cool. Chop shrimps, put them in a pan with eggs and butter, add mustard and seasoning, stir till mixture thickens. Add hake. Use cold.

*I find the following recipe really fishy, since it teams bacon with sardines. More than four people may enjoy this dish, since it seems right for cocktails or breakfast.*

**Devils on Horseback**

4 rashers streaky bacon
1 level teasp curry powder
8 sardines
4 slices fried bread

Cut each rasher of bacon in half and spread thinly with curry powder made to a paste. Wrap each piece of bacon round a sardine, bake and serve on fried bread.

*And here's a snack for VIPs:*

**Salmon Slices**

puff pastry
3oz cooked fresh salmon
½ teasp tarragon vinegar
1 small teasp paprika pepper
1 tabsp thick white sauce
egg white to glaze
parsley

Cut pastry into thin slices, 3½ x 1½in. Mash salmon with fork, mix well with all ingredients and sandwich between pastry slices. After baking, brush with egg white, and garnish with parsley.

*A salmon snack, but here's a fish course:*

**Breton Scallops**

12 scallops
2 tabsp butter
2 shallots
salt and pepper
3 tabsp white wine
1 tabsp minced parsley
2 tabsp fresh bread crumbs
browned crumbs
melted fat

Cut scallops into small pieces, making sure that the black intestines are removed. Chop white and coloured meat. Melt the butter in a pan. Add finely chopped shallots. Season. Stir in some parsley, fresh white crumbs and wine. Simmer uncovered for 8 min. Add more wine if too thick or more crumbs if too thin. Put into scallop shells, then sprinkle browned crumbs and melted fat over them. Brown under grill or in very hot oven.

*Turbot is about as scarce as lobster nowadays, but here's another splendid fish course. Please note that being a Northerner, Hilda means ¼pt when she mentions a gill as a measure.*

**Turbot Hollandais**

4 turbot steaks (1½lb)
1 small onion
2 teasp minced parsley
1 bay leaf
4 rashers streaky bacon
1 gill (¼pt) milk
½oz butter or margarine
½oz plain flour

Put the fish, cut side up, in a greased dish. Sprinkle with the minced onion and parsley. Place a piece of bay leaf on each steak; cover with rashers of bacon. Cook in a moderate oven for 40 min. Remove the bacon and discard the bay leaf, also the onion and parsley. Keep fish warm. Make the liquid from the dish up to ½pt with milk. Melt the fat in a saucepan and add flour. Make sauce with the liquid. Pour the sauce round the fish. Crisp the bacon under the grill; arrange this with garnish around the dish. If liked, 2oz of sauté mushrooms may be added to the sauce.

# 16
# Let Them Eat Cake

There is no doubt that cake making was Hilda's speciality. She made cakes in great variety, and her chocolate cakes were outstandingly successful. When we were at Thornhaugh she used to make a super cake containing Chocolate Menier. It was baked in a deep tin, and had no filling—it was just chocolate covered.

That cake is linked with the name of a Thornhaugh guest called Peter Buxton. Whenever he was staying Hilda made him two of the cakes, one to eat during his visit, the other to take home.

I don't think Hilda's chocolate cake ever brought this young fellow out in spots, but my brother-in-law remembers him as a measles case when he was a young boy. He remembers two measles cases. Peter had a friend staying with him and both boys caught it.

They were put into the bachelor wing, and brother-in-law Victor looked after them. Each day he negotiated an archway in which a blanket sprayed with disinfectant was hanging, to deliver their meals.

I am sure that Master Buxton would have approved the following cake, another of Hilda's excellent recipes.

## Chocolate Cake (Hilda's Special)

4oz margarine
4oz caster sugar
1 tabsp syrup—measure carefully
5oz self-raising flour
1½oz chocolate powder
1 or 2 eggs

Cream margarine, sugar and syrup till light and soft. Sieve all dry ingredients together. Beat eggs. Stir eggs and chocolate/flour mixture into margarine and syrup, just enough to make soft consistency, *not too soft* or it will sink! Bake 20-25 min at 400°F.

Fill with chocolate butter cream and cover with chocolate icing.

## Chocolate Fridge Cake

3 tabsp drinking chocolate
2 tabsp caster sugar
2oz butter
1 tabsp milk
½pt scalded and chilled evaporated milk
1 oz gelatin
Sponge fingers

Put chocolate, sugar, butter and tablespoon of milk in a pan. Melt until thick. Whip the evaporated milk, add to mixture; then add gelatin. Line tin with waxed paper. Put into tin alternate layers of chocolate mixture and sponge fingers. Chill 4 hours, decorate with whipped cream and grated chocolate and chopped nuts.

*If that's not rich enough for young guests, try:*

## Paradise Cake

Line a sandwich tin with short pastry

*Filling*
4oz margarine
4oz sugar
1 egg
4oz sultanas
2 tabsp each of:
  chopped cherries
  walnuts
  ground almonds
  semolina
  apricot jam

Spread the jam on the pastry. Cream margarine and sugar, add egg, then other filling ingredients, and spread over jam. Bake 40 min in moderate oven. Cool, cut into fingers and sprinkle with sugar

**Coffee Walnut Cake**

4oz margarine or butter
4oz sugar
8oz self-raising flour
1½oz walnuts
1 tabsp coffee essence
2 eggs
milk

*Topping*
½oz margarine or butter
1oz flour
½oz sugar
½oz walnuts

Rub fat into flour, add sugar and nuts. Mix to dropping consistency with coffee, eggs and milk. Pour into a 7in tin. Make topping: rub margarine into flour, add sugar and nuts. Sprinkle on top of cake. Bake at 375°F for 1½ hours.

**Gateau aux Marrons**
(All-in-one cake)

6oz soft margarine
6oz caster sugar
3 large eggs
6oz self-raising flour, sieved with 1½ level teasp baking powder
4oz chestnut purée

Place all in a bowl at the same time. Beat with a wooden spoon. Divide into two tins and bake at 325°F for 35-40 min.

*Filling*
2oz caster sugar
½pt cream
2oz chestnut purée

Whip together until stiff. Fill cake with half, cover top with remainder.

**Coffee Marshmallow Spread**

1 egg white
1 tabsp syrup
coffee essence

Whisk egg white and syrup over hot water till thick. Add coffee essence. Use as required.

*I was delighted to find Hilda's ice cream recipe, the delicious ice cream she used to make with the machine at Rise.*

**Ice Cream with Eggs**

2 eggs
1pt milk
4oz sugar
1/4oz gelatin (leaf gelatin, as always)
flavouring

Whisk the eggs well. Stir in the milk, add sugar. Cook in double boiler until thick. Remove, add gelatin, stir and strain into mixture. Add flavouring, and, when cooled, freeze.

With vanilla ice cream, fresh fruit may be served.

*For dessert, Hilda could be relied upon for a selection from her tremendous repertoire of sweets and puddings.*

**Cold Caramel Soufflé**

1/2pt milk
2 eggs
1oz cornflour
1oz gelatin
18 lumps of sugar
water
whipped cream

Make custard with egg yolks and cornflour. Cool, add dissolved gelatin, beat egg whites stiff and fold into custard. Pour into soufflé dish and set. Boil sugar in 1/2pt water until golden. Add 2 teasp cold water. Stir well, stand till cold. Pour over soufflé. Cover with whipped cream.

**Frangipane Tart**

short pastry to line a flan ring set on a baking tray
1 tabsp lemon curd
4oz margarine
4oz caster sugar
2 eggs
3oz plain flour
2oz ground almonds
almond essence

Spread lemon curd on the pastry. Cream margarine and sugar till fluffy. Beat eggs in one at a time. Fold in flour, almonds and essence. Spread over curd, place narrow strips of pastry over the top. Bake at 370°F for 45 min.

**Butterscotch Parfait**

1oz butter
3oz demerara sugar
¼pt water
4 eggs
½pt cream or evaporated milk
vanilla essence

Melt butter and sugar in a pan and boil 1 min. Add water and beat until butterscotch has dissolved. Beat the eggs and add to the butterscotch gradually. Add vanilla. Cook lightly for 5 min. Cool, then fold in whipped cream or evaporated milk.

**Caramel Parfait**

4oz granulated sugar
¼pt water
4 eggs
½pt cream

Put the sugar and water in a pan to boil. Meanwhile whip egg yolks. When the sugar and water are at thread consistency, add to whipped yolks. Whip cream and fold in. Whip egg whites and fold in. Pour into individual glasses and chill in refrigerator.

Perhaps around the time that some of these recipes were entered in Hilda's notebook, my husband and I were involved in supplying sweets for the young. We had a shop at Tur Langton in Leicestershire. One day a lady who lived in a large old house at Kibworth, a village nearby, passed on her way home from the hunt, riding side-saddle. Two small boys, interested in buying sweets, were in the shop.

Their fascination with licorice bootlaces and gob stoppers was interrupted as the lady went by. The side of the horse where her legs were was not visible to the shop.

One of the lads, about four years old, exclaimed: 'Ee, look! A woman wi' no legs, riding a oss.'

# 17
# A Legacy of Know-How

My brother-in-law treasures Hilda's cookery books. He uses them frequently, and keeps to her principles. During her last illness, when she realised she would not recover, she encouraged him to cook, and try making as many different dishes as possible.

This thoughtfulness was wonderful, considering she was so ill. I am amazed at the amount of cooking he does. Few men left alone could cope as he does, or cook to his standard, never having previously done any.

Hilda told me many times that she wanted to be sure that he could look after himself. I wonder if he would make the more elaborate of the recipes which follow, which are for special company. I should not be surprised.

**Guinea Fowl Casserole**

2 fowl
1oz margarine or butter
5oz onion
3oz mushrooms
4-5oz rice
salt, pepper, stock

Melt margarine, add onion. Fry for 4 min. Stir in rice, fry till light brown. Season well, add stock. When boiling well pour into oven dish. Stand fowl on the rice, cover dish and cook in oven for 1-1½ hours (¾ hour at 380°F and then at 300°F until tender). Dish birds on rice surrounded by stuffed tomatoes, mushrooms and rice. Serve with potato balls, fried.

**Stuffed Tomatoes**

8 tomatoes, hollowed out
2oz onion
2oz mushrooms
2oz cooked rice
2oz margarine
1oz chopped walnuts

Fry onion, mushrooms, rice and walnuts in margarine. Season and add 3 tabsp tomato pulp. Mix well and fill tomato shells. Bake 15 min at 300°F.

**Indian Eggs**

The following is extravagant, but it has the advantage that it can be served hot or cold, not necessarily in a silver dish!

1 poached egg per person
rice
cream
curry powder
salt and pepper
lemon juice to taste
sultanas
almonds
mango chutney
cayenne
butter

Arrange eggs in a silver dish. Whip the cream, mix in the curry, seasoning and lemon juice. Pour over the eggs. Fry some sultanas in a little butter, also some chopped almonds. Add a little chopped mango chutney sprinkled with cayenne pepper. Boil the rice as for curry, place the rice around the eggs with the sultana and nut mixture on the top of the rice.

**Chicken James**

(Perhaps my brother-in-law would rename this Chicken Victor!)

1 chicken
½pt dry white wine
2oz margarine or butter
1 tabsp oil
5-6 small onions, chopped
3 rashers bacon
4oz mushrooms
little cream

Melt fat and oil, brown chicken, do not cook. Remove from pan, add chopped onion. Cook a little, put chicken in casserole. Put the rashers of bacon on breast. Add all ingredients except cream and mushrooms, and cook till tender. Cook mushrooms in a little milk or the stock from chicken. Add the cream, pour over chicken.

*My brother-in-law recommended the following recipe, brought from the Continent. Hilda got it from Mr Brotherhood. Not being a particularly fit man, he used to go to Switzerland twice a year. He was very fond of sweetbreads and one time brought back this recipe.*

**Braised Sweetbreads**

sweetbreads
carrots
leek
onion
celery
1 bay leaf
a little thyme
few peppercorns
little meat glaze (or Bovril)
stock
arrowroot
sherry

Blanch sweetbreads. Fry all vegetables and herbs, add meat glaze, sweetbreads and stock. Cook in oven till tender. Remove sweetbreads, strain stock, thicken with a little arrowroot and sherry. Pour over sweetbreads in serving dish.

**Poulet de Grand Velouté**

1 chicken

*For stock*
bunch of herbs
1-2 carrots
leeks
onions stuck with cloves
celery
seasoning
clove of garlic

Simmer stock ingredients in water 20 min. Bring to fast boil. Put in chicken cut in four portions, bring to the boil, then simmer 15 min. Prepare Béchamel sauce from stock. Add a little nutmeg, pour over chicken. Serve with pilaff of rice.

**Pilaff of Rice**

6oz rice
1½oz butter
1 tabsp chopped onion
1pt light stock
pinch of saffron
seasoning
2 doz stoned raisins
1 doz shredded almonds

Melt half the butter in a saucepan. Add finely chopped onion, cook few minutes. Add rice and stir with a spoon until it is well coated with butter but not brown. Add the remainder of ingredients except the other half of the butter, cover saucepan and cook about ½ hour. When rice is tender but unbroken, add remainder of butter. Mix all lightly with a fork. This may be served with hot meat dishes, or with hard-boiled eggs.

**Liver Shaslik**

1lb liver (calf's lamb's or pig's)
2 medium size onions

8 tomatoes
1lb mushrooms
bay leaf
oil, vinegar, salt and pepper
1 lemon
parsley

Wash liver, remove pipes and dry. Cut into slices 1½in thick. Slice onions, cut tomatoes. Wash mushrooms; if large ones, halve them. Use eight large skewers. Thread on skewers in order: bay leaf, liver, mushroom, tomato, onion. Repeat until all is used. Put in the bottom of the grill pan, brush with oil and vinegar and leave ½ hour to marinate. Grill for 10 min. Put on hot dish. Add a little water to the pan. Boil hard on the stove top to reduce liquid. Add chopped parsley and lemon juice. Pour over meat. Serve with rice, mashed potato and vegetable.

*A recipe for breakfast:*

**Devilled Drumsticks**

cooked chicken drumsticks
made mustard
Worcester sauce
tomato purée
few drops of Tabasco (very hot)

Score chicken drumsticks across, and rub made mustard into the scores. Make a sauce with chicken stock and the Worcester sauce, tomato purée and Tabasco. Pour over drumsticks in dish and cook 30 min in moderate oven.

*And a recipe for lunch:*

**Chicken Croquettes**

1oz butter
1oz flour
½pt chicken stock
lemon juice
4oz minced chicken
2oz minced ham
1oz minced mushrooms
1 tabsp cream
pastry

Roll some pastry fairly thinly and stamp into rounds 3-4in in diameter. Mix all other ingredients together. Wet round the edges of pastry with brush. Put small portion of chicken mixture in the middle of each round and double over, pressing edges firmly together. Egg and breadcrumb the croquettes and fry to golden brown. Serve with hot sauce or salad.

*I imagine Victor might use these quick recipes when he has spare cheese:*

**Cheese Pudding**

4oz white breadcrumbs
1 chopped onion
1pt milk
2oz margarine or butter
2 eggs
6oz cheese
salt, pepper, mustard

Soak the breadcrumbs in the milk, with the chopped onion, for ½ hour. Add salt, pepper, melted fat and a little made mustard, two beaten egg yolks and then the grated cheese. Whip egg whites and fold in. Bake in oven, 400°F for 40 min. Lower heat half way through cooking time.

**Welsh Rarebit**

1oz butter
milk
½oz flour
4 tabsp grated cheese
salt
cayenne pepper
made mustard

Melt butter, gradually add flour, cook a few minutes. Add enough milk to make a thick paste. Add seasonings, cheese and mustard. When all mixed and creamy put on toast and grill.

**Irish Rarebit with Onion**

Lay slices of fried onion on top of Welsh Rarebit after grilling, or thin slices of tomato before grilling.

*Hilda included in her handwritten cook book some recipes for drinks. My father contributed his recipe for ginger wine, which he used to make every Christmas. It was too hot for the children, so we were given raspberry cordial. Hilda's 'Gingerette' is not quite so fierce as father's wine:*

**Gingerette**

2 dessertsp essence of ginger
4 dessertsp lemon essence
3 dessertsp essence of cayenne
3 dessertsp burnt sugar
4lb lump sugar
1oz citric acid

Pour first four ingredients over sugar and add 4 quarts of boiling water. When cold, add citric acid, previously dissolved in water. Stir and bottle. Drink 3 tabsp to a tumbler of water, cold in summer and hot in winter.

**Lemonade**

2lb granulated sugar
grated rind and juice of 2 oranges and 2 lemons
½oz tartaric or citric acid
2 quarts boiling water

Put grated rinds and juice of fruit with acid into a bowl with the sugar. Pour over this the boiling water, stir until dissolved, stand for 12-24 hours, then bottle.

**Hilda's Cowslip Wine**

Utensils needed include a quart jug for measuring two jugfuls of cowslip flower heads picked on a fine day. Fill the jug with them loosely, don't pack them in. Wash well.

You'll also need three pounds of granulated sugar, half an ounce of yeast, a lemon, and a gallon of water (boiling!).

Put the flower heads into a suitably sized bowl, pour the boiling water over them and stir well. Cover and leave for ten days. Strain off the liquid into another bowl. Add the thinly sliced lemon and sugar and stir well.

Spread the yeast on a slice of toast, and float on top of the liquid. Cover again and leave for three days. Remove the toast, strain and bottle. After a few weeks drop a toffee-sized piece of sugar candy into each bottle.

Three months after picking the cowslips, the wine is ready for drinking. It's even nicer if you keep it longer. Drink up soon after opening, or you'll lose the bouquet.

**Hilda's Sloe Gin**

9oz sloes
Half bottle of gin
4½oz sugar
Few drops almond essence

Prick the sloes to extract the juice and put all the ingredients into a large bottle. Shake the bottle every day for a month. At the end of the month empty the debris of the sloes. Leave for one more month, shaking every two or three days.

For an extra kick you can add a glass of brandy. The result is a drink that's pink and potent.

# 18
# Postman's Knock

We're back in the firelight. In spite of all the fire-laying, raking of ashes, brass and steel fire-iron cleaning and arm-stretching mantelpiece dusting she had to do in the big houses, Eileen Balderson still prefers a coal or wood fire to gas or electricity in her own home.

Husband Jack built the fireplace, and he enjoys the fire's warmth and light with her. But he's a countryman even more than he's a handyman. They share a heartfelt appreciation of the English countryside.

If Jack sees a pair of phantom animal eyes staring at him from a shadowy corner of the room he will be remembering a fright which will last him for his lifetime.

He was helping his father to round up stock in a field at three o'clock on a dark morning. The beasts were to be driven on foot to the station nearby, to be sent by rail to market. There was a strong, persistent wind, and a fitful moon with clouds boiling over it. Visibility came and went. He was trying to locate the beasts in order to get them through the gate of the field.

Suddenly something moved immediately in front of him. He had almost stepped on it. The creature reared itself on its hind legs. A pair of malevolently shining eyes were directed at him.

He yelled something—he can't remember what—and the animal made off. It was a huge fox, the biggest he had ever seen, and Jack was trembling with fright. He was about ten when that happened.

He was paid 1s 6d for being a cattle drover, and the money went to his mother, who had four other children besides himself to look after.

Their house was on a farm of 33 acres, part of a big estate. 'It was quite commonplace when having dinner to see from our windows the fox chased by the hounds and hunters in full cry. The fields fell away to a small valley, then rose again to a fir wood at the top of a hill, giving us a marvellous view.'

He and the other children spent a lot of time in the woods where there was an abundance of wild life, including deer. It was a wonderful place for wild strawberries and blackberries, and the biggest mushrooms ever.

'We knew a pear tree in a hedge, and used to take home pears in September in a clothes basket. They were as hard as iron, but by Christmas the juice ran down our chins.'

Jack had a happy childhood on an estate, roaming the fields and woods. He knew where all the wood pigeons' nests were. The young were known as squeakers, and he used to take some home about the time they were ready to fly. They did not fly into the pot, but they were delicious when cooked.

Mole catching earned Jack a few shillings. He got 9d a skin. He took a fox out of a snare and got 5s for the skin. 'What a pity it wasn't the fox that scared me that dark morning, I would have got 10s for him!' When a shoot was held he got 6d a day for beating.

His father got him a job cleaning boots at the big house on the estate, Scotten Hall, Stamford, Lincolnshire. This was a morning job and all day Saturday, for a wage of half a crown a week. When he left school he became full time hall boy for 8s a week.

Like Eileen he was impressed by the quietness of a big house. 'The silence might be broken by the rattle of pots and pans, but you were more likely to hear the lovely sound of the rooks.'

He had a pet jackdaw who went everywhere with him, and he fed the bird on rabbit livers. Another pastime of Jack's was rabbiting (on the jackdaw's behalf) with his gentleman's wire-haired terrier, Bogey. Whenever the animal's owner wanted the dog, it was with 'that damned boy'!

He heard his first radio programme at a garden fête in the grounds in 1922. It was a Gecophone with a horn speaker, and atmospherics spoiled the demonstration. The house's DC electricity system was by no means wireless. The wires went from the engine house to another outhouse full of large glass accumulators. A chauffeur taught him how to make a crystal set, and he is still a radio enthusiast. He and Eileen listen to classical music together, Eileen remembering Hilda's operatic arias.

Jack helped the gamekeeper with the rearing of pheasants. A thousand were raised in a season. They were reared under broody hens, and fed on raisins and wheat. 'They didn't get all the raisins. I had quite a few!' says Jack.

He enjoyed the days when the local hunt met at the house, and helped to serve drinks to the riders, keeping a wary eye on any horse with a yellow ribbon on his tail, indicating that he was liable to kick.

Children started hunting at an early age, with a groom in charge. There was jubilation if one of the children brought home a brush.

Jack and Eileen share a love of animals. Ring them, and their dog will answer the telephone before Eileen does. His friendly bark is heard before Eileen's pleasantly modulated tones.

It was not a telephone call, but a knock on the back door which was the start of happiness for Eileen.

She opened the door to Jack, who after a time in the army had become a postman. She had previously only exchanged 'Good mornings' with him, but he said (as boldly as he dared) 'How about it? Let's be friends.'

And Eileen asked him in for a cup of coffee.

# Index